FLOWER
DRUM
SONG

FLOWER
DRUM
SONG

Music by Richard Rodgers
Lyrics by Oscar Hammerstein II
Book by David Henry Hwang

Based on the original book by
Oscar Hammerstein II and Joseph Fields
Based on the novel by C. Y. Lee

THEATRE COMMUNICATIONS GROUP
NEW YORK
2003

This publication is made possible in part with funds from
the New York State Council on the Arts, a State Agency.

TCG books are exclusively distributed to the book trade by Consortium Book Sales
and Distribution, 1045 Westgate Dr., St. Paul, MN 55114.

The Broadway cast recording of *Flower Drum Song* is available through
DRG Records Incorporated, www.drgrecords.com.

Library of Congress Cataloging-in-Publication Data
Hwang, David Henry, 1957–
Flower drum song / music by Richard Rodgers ;
lyrics by Oscar Hammerstein II ; book by David Henry Hwang.
p. cm.
"Based on the original by Oscar Hammerstein II and Joseph Fields;
based on the novel by C.Y. Lee."
ISBN 1-55936-222-7 (Paperback : alk. paper)
1. Chinatown (San Francisco, Calif.)—Drama. 2. San Francisco
(Calif.)—Drama. 3. Chinese American women—Drama. 4. Women
immigrants—Drama. I. Rodgers, Richard, 1902–Flower drum song.
II. Lee, C.Y., 1917–Flower drum song. III. Title.
PS3558.W83 F58 2003
812'.54—dc21   2003004055

Cover imagery courtesy of Serino Coyne
Cover design by Kitty Suen
Book design and composition by Lisa Govan

CONTENTS

SPECIAL THANKS

To all who worked to make this American Dream come true, including the following who are not credited elsewhere in these pages: Mary Rodgers Guettel, the late James Hammerstein, Ted Chapin, Oskar Eustis, Chay Yew, my family (Kathryn, Noah and Eva) and those actors who gave their time and energy to developmental workshops of this script.

—D.H.H.

INTRODUCTION

By David Henry Hwang

As a young Chinese American growing up in Los Angeles in the 1960s, I developed a curious habit: if I knew a movie or TV show featured Asian characters, I would go out of my way *not* to watch it. This was a time when Asian characters in American popular culture were consistently inhuman: either inhumanly bad (Fu Manchu, Japanese soldiers) or inhumanly good (Charlie Chan, Asian ingénues who died for the love of a white B-movie actor). There was also the cook on *Bonanza*, but he didn't exactly qualify as a role model.

Then, while in my early teens, I was introduced to the 1961 film version of Richard Rodgers and Oscar Hammerstein II's *Flower Drum Song* on some late-night television broadcast. The encounter left me pleasantly shocked. Here was a show about love and culture clash in San Francisco's Chinatown, about romances between Asian men and women who spoke without accents, singing and dancing to beautiful and jazzy songs like "I Enjoy Being a Girl," "Grant Avenue" and "You

Are Beautiful." For Baby Boomers like myself, this was nothing short of revolutionary.

My attitude toward that work changed, however, when I began writing plays as a college student in the late 1970s. Along with other writers of color, we Asian Americans sought to define our own identities, rather than permitting those images to be drawn by mainstream society, which had done such a poor job of portraying us in my youth. As part of this movement, we rather simplistically condemned virtually all portrayals of Asian Americans created by non-Asians. So I ended up protesting *Flower Drum Song* as "inauthentic," though the show remained a guilty pleasure for many of us.

Almost two decades later, while watching the 1996 Broadway revival of *The King and I* by Rodgers and Hammerstein, I found myself struck by that production's desire to recreate authentically the Siamese setting of Anna and the King, and began remembering *Flower Drum Song*. By this point, the show (produced on Broadway in 1958) had fallen off the cultural radar, regarded as quaint, patronizing and old-fashioned. Yet the work loomed large for many Asian Americans: the 1961 film was the first movie released by a major Hollywood studio about and starring Asian Americans to reach a wide audience, a feat that would not be repeated until *The Joy Luck Club* in 1993.

As a playwright, I find that much of my work has involved a search for authenticity; if I could discover more truthful images to replace the stereotypical ones of my youth, perhaps I could also begin to understand my own identity. As part of this exploration, I have often taken older stories and reinvented them on my own terms. My best-known play, *M. Butterfly*, for instance, married Puccini's opera *Madama Butterfly* to the real-life story of a French diplomat who had a twenty-year affair with a Chinese actress, only to learn that his lover was actually a man.

So perhaps it was natural that I began to wonder if it might be possible to create my own version of *Flower Drum*

Song. I admired Rodgers and Hammerstein's ambition to write a musical about America through the eyes of Asians, who even today tend to be regarded as perpetual foreigners. And notwithstanding shows like *Miss Saigon* and *Pacific Overtures*, which are set overseas, *Flower Drum Song* has long stood alone as the only Broadway musical ever produced about Asian Americans. Could I aspire to write the book that Hammerstein might have wanted to write had he been Asian American, to respect the tone and spirit of the original while adding my own perspective? Could I re-envision the musical in a way that would feel relevant and moving to more culturally sophisticated, contemporary audiences?

I took my idea to the Rodgers and Hammerstein Organization, which accepted it. I also obtained the blessing of C. Y. Lee, the author of the groundbreaking 1957 novel of the same title (on which the musical was based), whose more bittersweet tone I hoped to capture in my new libretto.

Having received the necessary permissions, I wrote a first draft of a new book that failed in the most important respect: it did not work as a libretto. I had gone into this project with some arrogance, not having bothered to school myself in the very specific craft of musical book writing. At that point, the Rodgers and Hammerstein Organization wisely put me together with the director Robert Longbottom and David Chase, our musical adapter and director, who gave me a two-year crash course in musical theatre. During this time the three of us set out jointly to realize my ambitions.

I had always hoped to juxtapose the jazzy Rodgers and Hammerstein nightclub numbers with the traditional form of Chinese opera, as a metaphor for culture clash. Setting these two very different styles in opposition would raise a question: can they be reconciled? Could the old be transformed to create something new?

We also knew we had to keep our show in the world of the late 1950s to early 1960s to make some of the songs work.

Our concept dovetailed with the historical reality of the Chop Suey Circuit, Cotton Club-like night spots featuring all-Asian revues that had flourished in major American cities from the 1940s to the 1960s and that also influenced Hammerstein and his co-librettist, Joseph Fields, in the creation of their book. Over time, we evolved the story of a rundown theatre in San Francisco's Chinatown, whose patriarch clings to his dreams of performing Chinese opera despite an ever-shrinking audience. The story of this theatre's transformation into a Western-style nightclub became a metaphor for assimilation. Our rewrite was so comprehensive that I don't think a single line remains from the original book.

I began work on the musical with the intention of creating a more "authentic" *Flower Drum Song*. Yet, as in so many earlier artistic journeys, I discovered the search for authenticity and identity to be more mysterious, complicated and rich than I had anticipated.

When I began writing *M. Butterfly*, for example, I knew very little about opera and considered Puccini's heroine, Cio-Cio-San, to epitomize the stereotype of the submissive Asian woman. Yet by the time the show opened, I had gained new respect for Puccini's work and intentions. In his own time, the composer had done something bold and progressive by making his Japanese heroine the virtuous character and rendering her American lover as the cad or villain. One era's cultural breakthroughs may calcify and become stereotypes through time. Culture is a living thing, constantly changing and evolving; intercultural work has always existed, as artists have incorporated new influences through migration, conquest and commerce.

In this light, as we explored *Flower Drum Song*, the very notion of authenticity and stereotyping became much more complex and elusive. Studying the nightclubs of this period, I came to appreciate the work of their performers. Among the cast members of our show was the actress Jodi Long, whose father, Larry

Leung, appeared in the original *Flower Drum Song* on Broadway, and with his wife worked the Chop Suey Circuit. Jodi showed us a video of her parents on *The Ed Sullivan Show*: after Ed Sullivan introduces them as coming "direct from China" (which was true of neither), they emerge in traditional dress, speaking pidgin Chinese. Jodi's father eventually takes off his Chinese robe to reveal a tuxedo, and her mother reveals a ball gown, leading into a jazzy dance number.

How do we judge this? Furthermore, how do we regard the jokes about laundries and restaurants and Confucius that were characteristic of the period? Jodi says her parents believed that they were subverting the societal stereotypes of their day. I have come to embrace that explanation; you cannot necessarily judge attitudes of earlier eras by today's standards. Moreover, I began to realize that one generation's breakthroughs often become the next generation's stereotypes.

When my parents arrived here from Asia in the 1950s, the stereotype of Asians was that of poor, uneducated manual laborers: waiters, gardeners, launderers. Chinese of that era might have fantasized, "If only someday people could think of us as educated and rich, all of our problems would disappear!" Today, those earlier stereotypes have largely been reversed. Now we tend to be regarded as too educated, too wealthy and raising the curve in math class. Obviously, neither extreme is accurate; stereotyping continues, even when the particulars change. Similarly, when the movies of Bruce Lee became popular in America, they presented a new way of looking at Asian men as empowered fighters; a decade later, however, everyone assumed we all knew kung fu.

As a result of these explorations, I have become less interested in seeking some Holy Grail of authenticity and more convinced of the need to create characters who burst from the page or stage with the richness, complexity and contradictions of real people.

At its core, a stereotype is bad writing: a one- or two-dimensional cutout devoid of humanity, and therefore prone to demonization. Whether one's characters are cooks, laundrymen, computer scientists or gangsters, if they are all well written, they will exude humanity, which is ultimately the most effective weapon against stereotypes, and the most visceral measure of authenticity.

In 1958, Rodgers and Hammerstein opened a musical that presented Asian Americans as a vital part of this country's great social experiment. In today's world, how people from the far corners of this earth gather together to become Americans remains as vital and relevant a question as ever. Perhaps the riddle of identity is not one that we are ever meant to answer definitively. Rather, it is by asking the question throughout our own lives, and over the course of generations, that we give meaning to our existence and assert our common humanity.

March 2003
New York City

This introduction was printed in a similar version in the Arts & Leisure section of the Sunday *New York Times*, October 13, 2002.

FLOWER
DRUM
SONG

PRODUCTION HISTORY

This version of *Flower Drum Song* was first produced by the Center Theatre Group of Los Angeles (Gordon Davidson, Artistic Director/Producer; Charles Dillingham, Managing Director) at the Mark Taper Forum, where it opened on October 14, 2001. It was directed and choreographed by Robert Longbottom; the supervising musical director was David Chase, who also provided the orchestrations and arrangements; set design was by Robin Wagner, costume design by Gregg Barnes, lighting design by Brian Nason, sound design by Jon Gottlieb and Philip G. Allen, musical direction by Charles duChateau, hair and wig design by Carol F. Doran and casting by Amy Lieberman and Tara Rubin. The associate producer was Madeline Puzo, the assistant director was Tom Kosis, the assistant choreographer was Darlene Wilson, the Chinese opera consultant was Jamie H. J. Guan and the production stage manager was Perry Cline. The cast was as follows:

MEI-LI	Lea Salonga
WANG	Tzi Ma
TA	Jose Llana
CHIN	Alvin Ing
LINDA LOW	Sandra Allen
HARVARD	Allen Liu
LIANG	Jodi Long
CHAO	Ronald M. Banks

ENSEMBLE   Charlene Carabeo, Rich Ceraulo,
                    Eric Chan, Marcus Choi,
                Michael Dow, Thomas C. Kouo,
            Keri Lee, Blythe Matsui, Jennifer Paz,
                Robert Pendilla, Chloe Stewart,
              Kim Varhola, Christine Yasunaga,
                    Susan Ancheta, Marc Oka

Flower Drum Song was produced on Broadway by Benjamin Mordecai, Michael A. Jenkins, Waxman Williams Entertainment, Center Theatre Group/Mark Taper Forum/Gordon David-son/Charles Dillingham, with Robert G. Bartner, Stephanie McClelland, Judith Resnick, Dragotta/Gill/Roberts, Kelpie Arts/Dramatic Forces, and by arrangement with the Rodgers and Hammerstein Organization. It opened at Broadway's Virginia Theatre on October 17, 2002. It was directed and choreographed by Robert Longbottom; the musical adaptation and direction was by David Chase, set design by Robin Wagner, costume design by Gregg Barnes, lighting design by Natasha Katz, sound design by Acme Sound Partners, orchestrations by Don Sebesky, musical coordination by Seymour Red Press, hair design by David Brian Brown and casting by Tara Rubin Casting and Amy Lieberman. The associate director was Tom Kosis; the associate choreographer was Darlene Wilson; the Chinese opera consultant was Jamie H. J. Guan; the technical supervisor was Arthur P. Siccardi; the general manager was

Nina Lannan Associates; the associate producers were Dallas Summer Musicals, Inc., Brian Brolly/Alice Chebba Walsh and Ernest De Leon Escaler; the marketing director was Lauren Doll; the marketing constultant was TMG-The Marketing Group; the press representative was Boneau/Bryan-Brown; and the production stage manager was Perry Cline. The cast was as follows:

MEI-LI	Lea Salonga
WANG	Randall Duk Kim
TA	Jose Llana
CHIN	Alvin Ing
LINDA LOW	Sandra Allen
HARVARD	Allen Liu
LIANG	Jodi Long
CHAO	Hoon Lee
ENSEMBLE	Rich Ceraulo, Eric Chan, Marcus Choi, Ma-Anne Dionisio, Emily Hsu, Telly Leung, J. Elaine Marcos, Daniel May, Marc Oka, Lainie Sakakura, Yuka Takara, Kim Varhola, Ericka Yang, Susan Ancheta, Robert Tatad

CHARACTERS

WU MEI-LI, a new immigrant from China, twenties

WANG CHI-YANG, a Chinese opera actor and immigrant to San Francisco, fifties

WANG TA, his Chinese American son, twenties

CHIN, an old family friend of the Wangs, sixties

LINDA LOW, a Chinese American showgirl, twenties

HARVARD, Chinese American male, twenties

MADAME RITA LIANG, a talent agent, forties

CHAO HAI-LUNG, male, a new immigrant, twenties

MR. CHONG, owner of the On Leock Fortune Cookie Factory

MR. LEE, a restaurant owner

ENSEMBLE: CITIZENS OF THE PEOPLE'S REPUBLIC OF CHINA, COMMUNIST PARTY MEMBERS, MEI-LI'S FATHER, SOLDIERS, REFUGEES, CHINESE OPERA COMPANY MEMBERS, IMMIGRANTS, SHOWGIRLS, CHORUS BOYS, A GHOST COUPLE, STAGE MANAGER, PHOTOGRAPHERS, REPORTERS, FACTORY WORKERS, EMIGRANTS, WARRIOR DANCERS, MAIDEN DANCER, WEDDING GUESTS AND RESIDENTS OF CHINATOWN

NOTE: Chinese names are listed here, and sometimes referred to in the text, in traditional Asian order: last name, followed by first and middle names.

SETTING

1960. China and San Francisco's Chinatown.

MUSICAL NUMBERS

Prologue

A Hundred Million Miracles	*Mei-li and Ensemble*

Act One

I Am Going to Like It Here	*Mei-li*
Jazz Bit	*Showgirls and Linda*
I Enjoy Being a Girl	*Linda*
You Are Beautiful	*Mei-li and Ta*
Grant Avenue	*Madame Liang, Linda, Harvard, Ta, Chin, Mei-li, Wang and Ensemble*
Sunday	*Ta*
I Enjoy Being a Girl (Reprise)	*Mei-li*
Fan Tan Fannie	*Linda and Ensemble*
Gliding Through My Memoree	*Wang and Ensemble*
A Hundred Million Miracles (Reprise)	*Mei-li and Ensemble*

Act Two

Chop Suey	*Wang, Madame Liang and Ensemble*
My Best Love	*Chin*

PROLOGUE

Mei-li, a Chinese girl in her twenties, appears in a pool of light. As she sings, she plays a flower drum, which she carries under one arm. Song—"A Hundred Million Miracles":

MEI-LI:

> My father says
> That children keep growing,
> Rivers keep flowing, too.
> My father says
> He doesn't know why
> But, somehow or other, they do.
>
> They do!
> Somehow or other, they do.
>
> A hundred million miracles,
> A hundred million miracles
> Are happening every day.
> And those who say they don't agree,

Are those who do not hear or see.
A hundred million miracles,
A hundred million miracles
Are happening
Every Day!

(The ensemble members enter.)

An idle poet makes words on a page,
Writes on a page with his brush.
A musical friend makes notes to blend
Suggested by an idle thrush.

ALL:

A hundred million miracles.

MEI-LI:

Then a young soprano who reads what they wrote,
Learns every note, every word,
Puts all they wrote in her lovely throat
And suddenly a song is heard!

ALL:

A hundred million miracles,
A hundred million miracles
Are happening every day.

MEI-LI:

A poem, a singer, and a tune

ALL:

Can fly together to the moon!

A hundred million miracles . . .

(The ensemble members become Chinese citizens on bicycles in the People's Republic of China.)

> In every single minute,
> So much is going on
> Along The Yellow River or The Tiber or The Don.
>
> A hundred million miracles . . .

MEI-LI:

> A little girl in Chungking,
> Just thirty inches tall,
> Decides that she will try to walk and nearly doesn't fall!

ALL:

> A hundred million miracles!
> A hundred million miracles,
> A hundred million miracles,
> A hundred million miracles
> Are happening every day!
>
> A hundred million miracles,
> A hundred million miracles
> Are happening every day.

(Chinese citizens become Communist Party Members, waving Chairman Mao's Little Red Book.*)*

PARTY MEMBERS:

> My father says
> The sun will keep rising
> Over the eastern hill.
> My father says
> He doesn't know why,
> But somehow or other it will.

It will!
Somehow or other it will.

A hundred million miracles,
A hundred million miracles
Are happening every day.
And those who say they don't agree,
Are those who do not hear or see.

(Mei-li's father enters, angered by the spectacle. Mei-li tries to stop him, but he won't be dissuaded: tearing his copy of the Little Red Book, *he tosses it to the ground in protest. The crowd falls upon him, and he is apprehended by soldiers as the crowd disperses.)*

ALL:

My father says
The sun will keep rising
The sun will keep rising
The sun will keep rising . . .

(Mei-li's father breaks free of his captors long enough to whisper a command to his daughter: "Go!" Then he's dragged off by soldiers, leaving Mei-li alone with her drum.

Mei-li escapes from China onto a boat headed for America with other Refugees. The Refugees speak, beginning with the one we will come to know as Chao.)

REFUGEE #1 (Chao): Though my body crosses the ocean in this cramped tomb, I keep my mind fixed on my new life to come.

REFUGEE #2: My child will be born in America, and will grow up without fear, for she will know neither famine nor war.

REFUGEE #3: When I can do what I want, no man will ever be my master. When I can say what I wish, my lips will only speak the truth.

REFUGEE #4: When I finally spot the American coastline, my lungs will be filled—with the sweet breath of freedom.

MEI-LI: Father, I carry your memory with me across the seas. I think I can survive whatever lies ahead—so long as I don't lose hope.

(Packed into the bottom of a steamer ship, the Refugees cross the Pacific in a harrowing journey.)

ALL:

California, U.S.A.

(The lights of San Francisco's Chinatown appear around them.)

MEI-LI:

My father says
That children keep growing,
Rivers keep flowing, too.
My father says
He doesn't know why
But, somehow or other, they do.

ALL:

They do!
Somehow or other, they do.

MEI-LI:

A hundred million miracles,

ALL:

> A hundred million miracles,
> A hundred million miracles,
> A hundred million miracles
> Are happening every day!

(The New Immigrants disperse into Chinatown. Mei-li walks toward an old building: The Golden Pearl Theatre.)

> In every single minute,
> So much is going on . . .

 **ACT ONE**

SCENE 1

The Golden Pearl Theatre, a dilapidated old Chinese opera house in San Francisco's Chinatown. In full costume, Wang Chi-Yang, a man in his fifties, and his son Ta, early twenties, perform a scene from the Chinese opera along with company members. Wang runs the opera company and plays the male lead, while Ta portrays the female ingenue.

Chin, a man upward of sixty, enters and interrupts the performance.

CHIN: Master!

WANG: Can't you see we're performing?

TA: Dad, there's no one in the audience!

WANG: Anyone can play to a packed house. To perform before an empty one, *that* requires talent.

CHIN: There is someone here to see you.

(Mei-li enters.)

MEI-LI: You are Master Wang Chi-Yang? *(Bowing before Wang)* My name is Wu Mei-li. I am the daughter of Wu Cheng-En.

WANG: Wu Cheng-En? My oldest friend from opera school?

MEI-LI: I am sorry to tell you . . . that my father has passed on to the world of spirits.

WANG: He was so young. He was meant to live in better times. Son, bring her some tea.

(Ta exits.)

(To Mei-li) You escaped from China?

MEI-LI: My father left me only your name and the address of this theatre: on Grant Avenue, in San Francisco. He told me you have achieved great success here in America.

WANG: I have?

MEI-LI: He received your letters.

WANG: Oh, of course! I have.

(Pause.)

We draw our biggest crowds on Saturdays!

CHIN: Last week, six people!

WANG: Mei-li, welcome to your new family. This is Uncle Chin—

MEI-LI: "Big-Ear Chin"? My father told me your big ears were a sign you would one day grow wealthy.

CHIN: Living here in America has somehow made them smaller.

WANG: And my son, Ta—

(Ta, now out of costume, enters with the tea.)

MEI-LI: Oh! As a man, you are so much more . . . convincing.

TA: I practice being a man in my spare time. Welcome to America, kid.

(Ta gives the tea to Mei-li.)

WANG *(To Ta)*: Why have you removed your costume?
TA: Dad, when are you going to get it? This theatre is dying!
WANG: Am I dead?
TA: I was just trying to say—
WANG: These dedicated artists—are they dead?
CHIN: Every day, my wife tells me, it's a miracle I'm still alive!

(All laugh.)

WANG: Silence! So long as we draw breath, the Peking Opera lives. Especially here, in this land of white devils and fake Chinese. If we give up the fight, then who? Who will remain, to keep our world from being washed away by Coca-Cola and Mickey Mouse?
TA: Look, you wanna *maybe* put some butts in those seats? Why don't you find a girl to play the girl?
WANG: Where am I supposed to find a girl?
CHIN: Mei-li's father was the finest opera teacher I have ever known.
WANG *(To Mei-li)*: Were you in his company?
MEI-LI: Of course. But I am hardly worthy to be considered—
TA: This is America, false modesty will get you no place. You've got the job.
MEI-LI: How do you know I'm good enough?
WANG: Finally, someone around here shows proper respect. Mei-li, have you ever performed *The Flower Boat Maiden*?
MEI-LI: My father taught it to me once. But that was a long time ago.
WANG: Your father once saw me in that opera—when I played it with Ta's mother. Perhaps the two of them are now watching us from heaven.

(Pause.)

Ta will teach you the role. If you can learn it well, you may have a future in this company. *(To Chin)* Things are looking up for us! Come, we must thank the gods for our good fortune.

CHIN: We will burn incense at the temples?

WANG: No, we will toast them with whiskey at the bars! *(To a company member)* Dismiss the audience!

(Wang exits with Chin and company, leaving Ta alone with Mei-li.)

MEI-LI: I'm sorry. I don't mean to take away your role.

TA: Will you stop apologizing? I've been waiting all my life to get out of that dress.

(He puts the robe on Mei-li.)

Now Dad can finally let me off the hook without losing his precious Chinese face. But he's gonna want you to be perfect.

MEI-LI: I'll do my best.

TA: By the way, you know how most jobs involve money? This one doesn't.

MEI-LI: I don't care. Joining a theatre is like finding a family.

TA: I could give you a job waiting tables on Nightclub Night.

MEI-LI: "Nightclub Night"?

TA: Every Friday, I get to turn this place into a nightclub. I stage all the shows—starring this amazing girl named Linda Low. Dad lets me 'cuz someone's gotta pay the bills. Chinese opera doesn't sell a lot of tickets around here.

MEI-LI: It doesn't matter. For the first time in years, I have a hopeful feeling.

TA: Take care of yourself, understand? If you need a place to stay, I'll talk to the girls at the club. You and I start work tomorrow, at noon. And wear a scarf, San Francisco can get cold at night.

(Ta exits.
Song—"I Am Going to Like It Here":)

MEI-LI:

I am going to like it here.
There is something about the place,
An encouraging atmosphere,
Like a smile on a friendly face.

There is something about the place,
So caressing and warm it is—
Like a smile on a friendly face,
Like a port in a storm it is!

So caressing and warm it is,
All the people are so sincere—
Like a port in a storm it is,
I am going to like it here!

(The next day. Ta enters and begins showing Mei-li opera moves.)

TA: Let's get started. First you do the mincing walk, then the stupid pose, then the nauseating giggle. Got it?
MEI-LI: You know, Ta, in China, those steps have different names.

(She repeats his sequence, adding additional flourishes.)

TA: The way you use the sleeves—almost makes me wish I could work them into a number for Nightclub Night.

19

MEI-LI: Why not? Ta, sometimes you seem a hundred percent Chinese. Then a moment later, you become a hundred percent American.

TA: So what does that make me? A hundred percent nothing?

MEI-LI: No. I think you are . . . a hundred percent both.

TA: Is that possible? Let's go on.

(They perform the dance.)

MEI-LI:

    All the people are so sincere,
    There's especially one I like.
    I am going to like it here.
    It's the father's first son I like!

    There's especially one I like,
    There is something about his face.
    It's the father's first son I like
    He's the reason I love the place.

(A jump forward in time. Mei-li's audition. Wang, entering with the company members, dances with Mei-li. Ta enters to watch. Mei-li dances beautifully, winning Wang's approval and passing the audition.)

WANG: Tonight, you will make your debut before an American audience! *(To Ta)* Nice work, son.

(Wang exits with the company members.)

TA *(To Mei-li)*: Thank you.

(Ta exits.)

MEI-LI:

> There is something about his face,
> I would follow him anywhere.
> If he goes to another place
> I am going to like it there!

SCENE 2

The theatre, Friday afternoon. Ta is rehearsing the Nightclub Night Showgirls for their performance that night; the male dancers look on.
Song—"Jazz Bit":

SHOWGIRLS:

> You be the rock
> I'll be the roll,
> You be the soup,
> I'll be the bowl.
> You be the furnace,
> I'll be the coal—rock, rock, rock!

(Spoken) And now, Miss Chinatown San Francisco . . . Linda Low!

(Ta awaits the entrance of Linda, who does not enter.)

TA *(Spoken)*: Linda? Linda!

You're late!	SHOWGIRLS *(Singing)*:
Linda, You're on!	You be the rock,
	She'll be the roll,
I've had it!	You be the soup,
That girl is out of	She'll be the bo-owl, co-oal—
this number!	
	So let's rock, rock, rock!

(Linda Low, twenties, enters and joins the Showgirls for the end of the number.)

LINDA AND SHOWGIRLS:
   Rock! Rock! Rock, rock!

LINDA: Sorry I'm late!
TA: I suppose you have a good excuse?
LINDA *(Showing off her dress)*: Yes, and I'm wearing it!
TA: Did you get that from some guy?
LINDA: Yeah, a guy named Christian . . . Dior.
TA: We were just running the first act finale.
LINDA: We've been doing that bit for months. It's the *new* number that you and I have gotta talk about.
TA *(To company)*: Take a break!

(Harvard, a man in his twenties, enters with a clothing rack.)

LINDA: Harvard! Gimme that moth-eaten old thing!
HARVARD *(Taking an old robe from the rack)*: I like to think of it as a charming native robe.
LINDA *(To Ta)*: You really expect me to wear *that*?
HARVARD: It's from the Chinese opera. If it was good enough for Ta to wear, it's good enough for you.
TA *(Embarrassed)*: Harvard! *(To Linda)* It's part of my concept for the number: a fresh off the boat maiden turns into an all-American girl. Just try it on, please?

(Linda exits with the robe. Wang and Mei-li enter in opera costume, along with Chin.)

WANG *(To Mei-li)*: How about a new production of *Lady White-snake*? Such a romantic story will fill our audience with young people.

CHIN: He means anyone under fifty.

(Wang notices the Showgirls rehearsing.)

WANG: What's going on, here?

TA: Don't start, Dad. You promised me five o'clock, and it's already 5:30.

WANG: When *we* rehearse, we do not even look at the clock.

TA: Well, *we* have to worry about an audience actually showing up. *(To Harvard and the company)* Get to work on those fittings! C'mon, guys!

(Harvard exits with the Showgirls.)

WANG: And I suppose *your* audiences are so large?

TA: Last week, almost fifty people.

WANG: Americans?

TA: You mean, *Caucasians?* Mostly.

WANG: Americans are so much more common in America. Fifty of your Americans are equal to six of my Chinese. *(To Mei-li)* I try to tell my son: the Americans will never accept him in their country.

TA: Maybe you oughta show up sometime. See for yourself if we're accepted.

WANG: No thank you!

TA: Afraid we might prove you wrong?

WANG: I have better things to do with my Friday evenings!

(Wang exits.)

CHIN *(To Ta, referring to Wang)*: It is two-for-one night at Trader Vic's.

(Chin exits.)

TA *(To Mei-li)*: Every week, he's gotta make a scene. Jeez!

MEI-LI: Why do you talk to him like that?

TA: Nothing I do is good enough for that man. What does he want from me?

MEI-LI: The only thing he wants is your respect.

(Linda enters, wearing the opera robe. She attempts to move the sleeves in the style of the Chinese opera.)

LINDA: Well, I guess this is sorta sexy—if you have a thing for Chinese grandmothers. How do these sleeves work again?

TA: Lemme show you.

MEI-LI: Actually, you can get them to flow more, if you move like this.

(Mei-li demonstrates.)

LINDA *(To Ta)*: You hired a sleeve specialist?

MEI-LI: My name is Wu Mei-li, I am the daughter of—

LINDA: I don't need your entire résumé, honey. Thanks for the tip.

TA: Mei-li inspired our new number.

LINDA: See, Ta? I always knew you were a Chinatown kid at heart.

TA: Hey, you're gonna love this dance. And someday, you might even learn to love me.

LINDA: I already do—

(Linda kisses Ta on the cheek. Mei-li watches them.)

—like a brother. Ta-ta, Ta.

(Linda exits. Ta drifts back toward Mei-li.)

TA: She's amazing, isn't she?

MEI-LI: She's certainly very healthy.

TA: Wait'll you see her dance. And she sings like a dream.

MEI-LI: And can she also strangle a chicken?

TA: She's probably not much of a cook. Not that I'd know. She dates mostly—you know—white guys.

MEI-LI: So have you asked her . . . to marry you?

TA: First we date, *then,* we marry.

MEI-LI: "Date"?

TA: It's a . . . courtship ritual.

MEI-LI: Like the old romantic legends!

TA: Where a guy takes a girl's hand—

MEI-LI: Looks into her eyes . . .

TA: And says— *(Breaking the mood)* Why don't you ask Linda?

MEI-LI: Sorry?

TA: She's the expert. On dating.

MEI-LI: In China, courtship is easy: you simply marry the man before he can get to know you.

TA: Well, over here, love can be long and agonizing. And when it comes to making men suffer, no one does it like Linda Low.

SCENE 3

The backstage dressing room. Linda rehearses with her sleeves, as Harvard watches.

HARVARD: Just keep practicing. You've already shamed your ancestors by working here. The least you could do is get the sleeves right.

(Mei-li, entering, knocks on the door.)

MEI-LI: Miss Low?

LINDA *(Sees Mei-li)*: Hi Chow Fun! Listen, could you show me again? This is a lot harder than it looks.

(Mei-li demonstrates the sleeves again.)

MEI-LI: In China, women train from childhood just to master the movement of the sleeves.

LINDA: Stripping refugees—what will Ta think of next?

HARVARD: These old Chinese costumes are amazing. When Europeans were still living in caves, our ancestors were already being fabulous.

(Harvard exits.)

MEI-LI: You mean on Nightclub Night . . . you take off your clothes?

LINDA: Gotta give those nice Caucasian boys a reason to stray far from Mommy. *(Noticing Mei-li's opera headdress)* God, that headdress thing must weigh a ton. How do you even stand up?

MEI-LI *(Noticing Linda's shoes)*: I was wondering the same about you.

LINDA: Oh, the heels? Let's face it: we Oriental girls don't have the longest legs.

MEI-LI: They are long enough to reach the ground. Ta tells me you are an expert in American ways.

LINDA: How would he know? He's hardly set foot outside Chinatown.

MEI-LI: Oh, but he knows so much about Chinese opera and Western nightclubs . . . and what to wear when it's cold at night.

LINDA: Really? If you think the boy's so great, why don't *you* date him?

MEI-LI: I did not mean—

LINDA: You get Ta off my back, and I'll help you!

MEI-LI: But I must first "date"? Is it going to be painful?

LINDA: Look, men have made us suffer for centuries. Dating is how we make them pay us back.

MEI-LI: But my mother told me that a woman's life is filled with misery.

LINDA: Mine told me the same thing. Look at this picture. Me—at age fifteen, in Seattle. Low Lee-Fung. My friends called me "Lowly." Then one day I realized—we're not in China anymore. No more stuffing daughters down a well, or selling us into slavery. And foot binding—what was *that* all about? No, this is the land of opportunity.

(Song—"I Enjoy Being a Girl":)

I'm a girl and by me that's only great!
I am proud that my silhouette is curvy,
That I walk with a sweet and girlish gait,
With my hips kind of swively and swervy.
I adore being dressed in something frilly
When my date comes to get me at my place.
Out I go with my Joe or John or Billy,
Like a filly who is ready for the race!

When I have a brand new hair-do,
With my eyelashes all in curl,
I float as the clouds on air do—
I enjoy being a girl!
When men say I'm cute and funny,
And my teeth aren't teeth, but pearl,
I just lap it up like honey—
I enjoy being a girl!

I flip when a fellow sends me flowers,
I drool over dresses made of lace,
I talk on the telephone for hours
With a pound and a half of cream upon my face!

I'm strictly a female female,
And my future, I hope, will be
In the home of a brave and free male
Who'll enjoy being a guy,
Having a girl like me!

(Harvard enters and drags Linda off to her performance onstage.)

(To Mei-li) You see? You can do it, too! You can become . . . his American Dream!

(The music from "I Enjoy Being a Girl" segues into underscoring, as we transition into:)

SCENE 4

Onstage. Nightclub Night. The stage is transformed into a Western-style nightclub. Ta enters, serving as the emcee.

TA: And now, that "All-American Chinese Dream"—Linda Low and her Fresh Off the Boat Dancers!

(Dressed in the Chinese opera robe, Linda and the Chorus Boys perform "I Enjoy Being a Girl." Linda utilizes the sleeve moves that Mei-li taught her.)

LINDA:

> I enjoy being a girl!
> I enjoy being a girl!
>
> I flip when a fellow sends me flowers,
> I drool over dresses made of lace,
> I talk on the telephone for hours
> With a pound and a half of cream upon my face!
>
> When I have a brand new hair-do,
> With my eyelashes all in curl,
> I float as the clouds on air do—
> I enjoy being a girl!
> When someone with eyes that smoulder,
> Says he loves every silken curl
> That falls on my ivory shoulder—
> I enjoy being a girl!
>
> When I hear a complimentary whistle
> That greets my bikini by the sea,
> I turn and I glower and I bristle—
> But I'm happy to know the whistle's meant for me!

(Linda strips down from the Chinese opera outfit to a bikini and dances with the Chorus Boys.)

> Oh, baby, that whistle's meant for me!

(The Showgirls enter and join Linda, becoming reflections in her mirror.)

> I'm strictly a female female,
> And my future, I hope, will be

In the home of a brave and free male
Who'll enjoy being a guy,
Having a girl like me . . .

SCENE 5

Backstage, after the show. Ta counts money with Harvard.

HARVARD: Four hundred sixty dollars and eighty-seven cents.
TA: We're up from last week!

(Mei-li enters as Harvard exits.)

Hey, *there* you are! What'd you think of the show?
MEI-LI *(Still overcome by the experience)*: It was so . . .
(Awkwardly imitates dance moves) When she took off
her—and marched around in those—and then started
shaking her—
TA: Calm down, you're gonna break something.
MEI-LI: The dance was really inspired . . . by me?
TA: Sure. Except for the naked part.
MEI-LI: I loved it.
TA: I've got all these ideas popping into my head—like a dance
for Linda and the boys—where they all come out swing-
ing their pigtails.
MEI-LI: Ta, Chinese consider the pigtails to have been a shame-
ful thing for men.
TA: But I need some prop she and the boys can use together.
MEI-LI: How about fans? They can be delicate, yet also very
masculine.

(Wang enters wearing a dragon head. He performs an exorcism ritual, running around the space to purify it from evil spirits, as Chin plays a portable gong.)

WANG: Demons begone! Demons begone!

TA: Dad! Why are you doing this?

WANG: Why? Because I finally came to see your Nightclub Night.

TA: What'd you think of the show?

WANG: To think my own son created this travesty!

TA: Yeah, I'm the director. And you're jealous.

WANG: Jealous?

TA: You heard something tonight that you haven't known in twenty years: the sound of applause.

WANG: Pah! Anyone can get white demons to applaud. All you have to do is put a Chinese girl onstage and take away her clothes.

MEI-LI: Master Wang, my father told me that when he first put women in the opera, you defended him. That you told the traditionalists, "Times have changed."

WANG: Well, now they have changed too much!

(Pause.)

This disgrace you call "Nightclub Night"—is over.

(Wang exits.)

CHIN *(To Ta)*: I thought the costumes were very pretty.

(Chin exits.)

TA: Soon as you think you're onto something great, it all comes crashing down around you.

MEI-LI: Ta, I want to show you something.

(Mei-li produces her flower drum.)

TA: A flower drum?

MEI-LI: As a child, my father was sent to sing for money in the streets. He was told to use this drum for begging. But he used it instead . . . for wishing.

TA: So you've had it since you were a kid?

MEI-LI: My father was arrested by the Communists—and died in prison. Before he went away, he whispered to me, "Take this drum, Daughter—and never stop dreaming. For the more you dream, the more miracles you will see."

TA: My mother died on the boat, coming to America. I was only two. And Dad never really talked much about her.

MEI-LI: My father saw them perform many times.

TA: Really? Were they good together?

MEI-LI: Their most famous performance was in *The Flower Boat Maiden*. Father said watching them was like seeing that opera for the first time, back when it was new.

TA: Must've been tough to breathe life into those corny old stories. The love of a beautiful maiden turns a humble scholar into a god. Sounds credible to me.

MEI-LI: Ta, the Flower Boat Maiden does not turn the scholar into a god. He has always been a god. Only he has forgotten that he came originally from heaven.

TA: So somehow—what?—she figures out his secret identity?

MEI-LI: She loves him. And that is enough. When he looks into her eyes, he realizes . . . that he has always been something more. You know the story . . .

(Song—"You Are Beautiful":)

Along the Hwang Ho Valley,
Where young men walk and dream—

> A flower boat with singing girls
> Came drifting down the stream.
>
> I saw the face of only one
> Come drifting down the stream . . .
>
> You are beautiful,
> Small and shy . . .

TA: I've never heard it that way before.

MEI-LI: My father always said, to create something new, we must first love what is old. Now sing it with your heart.

TA:

> You are beautiful,
> Small and shy,
> You are the girl whose eyes met mine
> Just as your boat sailed by.
>
> This I know of you,
> Nothing more.
> You are the girl whose eyes met mine,
> Passing the river shore.
>
> You are the girl whose laugh I heard,
> Silver and soft and bright,
> Soft as the fall of lotus leaves
> Brushing the air of night.
>
> While your flower boat
> Sailed away,
> Gently your eyes looked back on mine,
> Clearly you heard me say:
> "You are the girl I will love some day."

(Mei-li begins performing a dance from The Flower Boat Maiden. *Ta finds himself joining her. A Ghost Couple appears upstage, performing the dance in Chinese opera costume, as it might have been done centuries ago, mirroring the movements of Mei-li and Ta.)*

TA:

You are the girl whose laugh I heard,
Silver and soft and bright,
Soft as the fall of lotus leaves
Brushing the air of night.

(The Ghost Couple disappears.)

TA AND MEI-LI:

While your flower boat
Sailed away,
Gently your eyes looked back on mine,
Clearly you heard me say:
"You are the girl I will love some day."

(They gaze upon one another. Suddenly, Ta takes Mei-li in his arms and kisses her. When they break apart, Ta is left feeling confused.)

TA: I'm sorry.
MEI-LI: You Americans—you apologize too much.
TA: I don't know what came over me.
MEI-LI: Perhaps the old stories are more powerful than you think.
WANG *(Offstage)*: Ta! Ta!

(Madame Rita Liang, forties, enters with Linda and Harvard. Wang and Chin are close behind.)

LIANG: Imagine! A prime piece of Chinatown real estate practically abandoned all these years. *(Sees Ta)* And you must be Wang Ta.

WANG *(To Ta)*: This lunatic burst right in. Please remove her from the premises!

TA *(To Liang)*: Sorry, but we're closed.

(Liang hands her card to Ta.)

LIANG: Madame Rita Liang—theatrical agent.

TA *(Reads the card)*: For "Oriental talent"?

LIANG: I've just signed your principal performer: Linda Low. Lucky girl. And I believe your club has enormous potential!

WANG: How can that be, when this nightclub is now closed!

LIANG *(To Ta)*: That man may be speaking English, but I have no idea what he's talking about.

TA: My father is a traditionalist.

LIANG *(To Wang)*: Honored Elder, I have made it my life's mission to improve the image of the Chinese people. So, you see? I too am a traditionalist. That number with the Chinese maiden turning into a fun-loving American girl—it was like an American dish made with Chinese ingredients—like Chop Suey—and people in this country just eat that stuff up.

TA: We've got all these ideas for new numbers!

LIANG: You'll need proper advertising, of course. Marketing. Outreach to the mainstream audience. Plus a small infusion of capital to class up the place. All of which I am willing to provide!

WANG: You talk as if you own this theatre.

LIANG: Master Wang, when the average American thinks of Chinatown, do you know what they imagine? Opium dens, Tong wars, female slavery and questionable cuts of meat.

WANG: Lies! Insults to the greatness of a—

LIANG: Exactly. Join with me and together, we can create . . . a
new Chinatown. We've got to show the Americans who
we really are. No more inscrutable Orientals, but smiling,
all-American faces. Polite men, beautiful women, the
finest cuisine in the world.

WANG: Sounds nice. Where can you find such a place?

(Song—"Grant Avenue":)

LIANG:

> On the most exciting thoroughfare I know.
> They call it—
>
> Grant Avenue, San Francisco, California, U.S.A.—
> Looks down
> From Chinatown
> Over a foggy bay.
>
> You travel there in a trolley, in a trolley up you climb—
> Dong Dong!
> You're in Hong Kong,
> Having yourself a time.
>
> You can eat, if you are in the mood,
> Shark-fin soup, bean cake fish.
> The girl who serves you all your food
> Is another tasty dish!
>
> You know you
> Can't have a new way of living till you're living all the
>   way
> On Grant Avenue

LINDA *(Joining in)*:
> Where is that?

LIANG:

> San Francisco,
> That's where's that!
> California,
> U.S.A.

WANG: This is nonsense! You actually believe you can change the way these white demons think?

LIANG: Why not? In America, all it takes . . . is the right pitch. *(She sings:)*

> A Western street with Eastern manners,
> Tall pagodas and golden banners
> Throw their shadows through the lantern glow.
> You can shop for precious jade or
> Teakwood tables or silk brocade or

LINDA:

> See a bold and brassy night club show,

LIANG:

> On the most exciting thoroughfare I know.
>
> They call it—
>
> Grant Avenue,

(Linda, Harvard and Ta join Liang, trying to persuade Wang.)

LINDA:

> San Francisco,

HARVARD:

> California,

TA:

    U.S.A.—

LIANG:

    Looks down
    From Chinatown
    Over a foggy bay.

LIANG, TA, LINDA AND HARVARD:

    You travel there in a trolley, in a trolley up you climb—

(Chin joins Liang's cause:)

CHIN:

    Dong Dong!
    You're in Hong Kong,
    Having yourself a time.

(So does Mei-li:)

MEI-LI:

    You can eat, if you are in the mood,
    Shark-fin soup, bean cake fish.

CHIN:

    The girl who serves you all your food
    Is another tasty dish!

LIANG:

    You know you

LIANG, TA, LINDA, CHIN, HARVARD AND MEI-LI:

    Can't have a new way of living till you're living all the
        way
    On

LIANG:

Grant Avenue

Where is that?

WANG:

San Francisco,

LIANG:

That's where's that!

ALL:

California,
U.S.A.

(During a musical interlude, Liang leads the company out to the streets and begins to remake the theatre, in a montage sequence that continually jumps forward in time. With workers and company members assisting her, they put up banners that read: NIGHTCLUB NIGHT: FRIDAY—ONE SHOW ONLY!)

LIANG: The first thing that's gotta go is that name. "Golden Pearl"? It's not even logical. Get rid of it!

(Workers take down a sign reading: THE GOLDEN PEARL THEATRE. Wang enters with his dragon head, attempting another exorcism.)

WANG: Demons begone! Demons begone!
LIANG *(Noticing the dragon head)*: Hey, I can use that! *(Taking the dragon head)* Makeup! *(Giving the dragon head to Harvard, who exits with it)*
WANG: No!

(Ta enters, rushes up to Liang.)

TA *(Spoken)*: We've already sold out the first show.

CHORUS BOYS *(Singing)*:
Grant Avenue,
San Francisco,
California,
U.S.A.
Looks down
From Chinatown

WANG *(Spoken)*: "First show"? I told you—one show only.

(Chanting through dialogue:)
Chinatown, Chinatown . . .

(Liang leads Wang downstage. As she speaks, the ONE SHOW ONLY! banner is replaced with SECOND SHOW ADDED!)

LIANG: Master Wang, do you believe in destiny?

WANG: Destiny is when things happen the way *I* want them to!

LIANG: But what we want can change. Old dislikes can disappear.

WANG: I don't like you. When are you going to disappear?

LIANG: Now listen and you can hear your ancestors telling you . . . your future has already been decided.

(Liang blows a whistle—the dragon head reappears, now gaudily refurbished and leading a promotional Grand Opening Parade. THE GOLDEN PEARL THEATRE sign has been replaced with a new neon marquee reading: CLUB CHOP SUEY! while workers add a new banner announcing the addition of a SPECIAL MIDNIGHT SHOW! Liang leads the parade with megaphone in hand:)

People of San Francisco, I come to you today with news of revolution—a revolution in entertainment! This Friday night, East and West will meet right here on Grant Avenue! You have nothing to lose but your old ways of living! So, hop aboard the New Chinatown Express!

(Chin appears as part of the parade, dressed as a cable car driver and carrying a placard reading: NEW CHINATOWN EXPRESS!*)*

CHIN:

Dong Dong!

ALL:

You know you
Can't have a new way of living till you're living all the
way
On

LIANG:

Grant Avenue

Where is that?

ALL:

San Francisco,
That's where's that!
California,
U...S...A...

SCENE 6

Wang inspects the new Club Chop Suey.

WANG: I cannot even recognize my own theatre any longer! That woman has destroyed five thousand years of Chinese culture.

(Chin enters, still wearing the cable car placard.)

CHIN: And in only four weeks!

WANG: And you—traitor!—take that sign off! I did not help you enter this country so you could march down Grant Avenue yelling: "Dong Dong!"

CHIN: I also yell: "Clang Clang."

(Chin exits. Mei-li enters in a waitress outfit.)

MEI-LI: Uncle Wang, have you seen Ta?

WANG: Why would I want to see Ta? He has betrayed everything I ever taught him!

MEI-LI: Perhaps he is *using* everything you ever taught him and all this is his tribute to you.

WANG: Next time he wants to pay tribute, tell him to buy me a watch!

(Wang exits, as Chao, twenties, enters, carrying a crate of fortune cookies.)

CHAO: I'm looking for Madame Liang—

MEI-LI: She's in the kitchen—

CHAO: Mei-li? *(Beat)* We came over together . . . on the boat?

MEI-LI: Chao? It's so good to see you.

CHAO: You got yourself a job—here? Do you take off your clothes?

MEI-LI: No, I'm a waitress!

CHAO: Good. I have a job as well. It's not much, but it's a start.

MEI-LI: It's a good start . . .

CHAO: Mei-li, I've been looking for you ever since we arrived here . . . and I was wondering if perhaps you would like to go to dinner with me—tonight?

MEI-LI: But the club is opening tonight.

CHAO: All right, then—tomorrow.

MEI-LI: Chao, I'm honored, but there is another . . . another man, who I—

42

(Ta enters, sees Chao.)

TA: Those fortune cookies were supposed to have gotten here hours ago. Where have they been?

MEI-LI: Ta.

CHAO: They took the boat. All the way from China.

MEI-LI: This is Chao Hai-lung. We traveled together to this country.

TA: Sorry if I lost my temper, it's a crazy day.

(He tosses Chao a coin.)

No hard feelings, OK?

(Chao tosses the coin back to Ta.)

CHAO: No hard feelings. *(To Mei-li)* Think about my offer, OK?

(Chao exits.)

TA: What's his problem? Did he make a pass at you?

MEI-LI: No, he only asked me out to dinner.

TA: You like him?

MEI-LI: Chao? No! I mean, not in that way . . . before I can date here, I still have so much to learn.

TA: What do you mean?

MEI-LI: The girls said, you can tell that a man is serious if he takes you to the Coconut Grove—

TA: Linda told you that—

MEI-LI AND TA: —or the Top of the Mark—

TA: Forget all that stuff. Every girl has her own appeal. A guy wouldn't expect to take someone like you to the Top of the Mark or the Coconut Grove or anyplace fancy at all.

MEI-LI: Should I be happy about that?

TA: Here's the kind of love I'd wish for you: when I was a kid, I used to daydream about what it'd be like to have a normal family—with a mom, and a dad who didn't walk around the house all day with his makeup on. I'd imagine them happy together, just doing nothing.

MEI-LI: And do you think such a love is possible . . . for me?

TA: Just wait. One day, that special guy will get down on one knee and say to you *(Sings)*:

(Song—"Sunday":)

> Now that we're going to be married,
> I keep imagining things,
> Things that can happen to people
> When they are wearing gold rings:

MEI-LI: Is that the "proposal"?

TA: Yes!

> Being together each morning,
> Sharing our coffee and toast—

MEI-LI: I prefer tea.

TA:

> That's only one of the pictures.
> Here's what I picture most:

> Sunday,
> Sweet Sunday,
> With nothing to do,

MEI-LI: Did we lose our jobs?

TA: No, it's our day off here.

Lazy
And lovely,
My one day with you,
Hazy
And happy,
We'll drift through the day.
Dreaming the hours away.

MEI-LI: What would we do all day?

TA:

While all the funny papers lie or fly around the place,
I will try my kisses on your funny face.

(He plays getting fresh with her.)

Dozing,
Then waking
On Sunday, you'll see
Only
Me!

(Mei-li winds up in Ta's arms. Music turns softer.)

You see, any guy in any country—wants a girl he can be
comfortable with, who makes him feel . . . like the man he
wants to be.

Sunday,
Sweet Sunday,
On Sunday, you'll see
Only . . .

(He kisses her.)

I've gotta stop doing that.

MEI-LI: I could not disagree with you more.
TA: But I don't want to hurt you.
MEI-LI: I am not afraid.
HARVARD (*Offstage*): Ta!

(*Harvard enters, panicked.*)

Ta! I can't go on, I'm a fake! I'm supposed to be playing this sailor who's been all over the world, when the truth is . . . I've never traveled south of San Jose!
TA: Hold it together, Harvard. We'll discuss this inside.

(*Harvard exits.*)

(*To Mei-li*) Look, after the show tonight, you and I have got to have a long talk, OK?

(*Ta and Mei-li exit separately.*)

SCENE 7

Linda's dressing room. She gets ready for the show as Liang watches.

LIANG (*Playing a reporter*): All right, let's try another one: "Miss Low, how long do you plan to continue performing at the Club Chop Suey?"
LINDA: Soon as Hollywood calls, I'm on the next bus to L.A.
LIANG: No, no!
LINDA: But that's the truth.
LIANG: They're reporters. We don't tell them the truth. Say: "I see this as a stepping-stone to my real career—as a future wife and mother." Then giggle.

(Liang covers her mouth and giggles like a geisha.)

LINDA: You really think all this could lead to the movies?

LIANG: Why not? I've packed the house with everything a girl needs to make it in show business: reporters, politicians, organized crime figures.

LINDA: Great. One day, everyone who's ever made fun of me will look up and see this face—twelve feet tall.

LIANG: Those legs, that figure—it's like looking at myself when I was young.

LINDA: You looked like this twenty years ago?

LIANG: Ten.

(Mei-li enters.)

MEI-LI: Linda!

LIANG: Not bad.

MEI-LI: Excuse me?

LIANG: I like the new waitress uniforms! *(To Linda, referring to Mei-li)* This one—she's just arrived from China, right?

LINDA: Yeah. Why?

LIANG *(To Mei-li)*: No spit or blow nose into food, OK?

(Liang exits.)

MEI-LI: Linda, Ta says he wants to tell me something important tonight. And he kissed me!

LINDA: Wow. Whoever invented the phrase "slow boat to China" never met you.

MEI-LI: Do you think he will say . . . that he loves me?

LINDA: Let's sweeten the bait— *(To offstage)* Harvard!

MEI-LI: This is either the most wonderful feeling on earth—or I've come down with a fever.

LINDA: Harvard!

(Harvard enters, half-dressed in a sailor's suit.)

HARVARD: Yes, my lord and master?
LINDA: Could you fetch my yellow dress from the closet?
HARVARD: Sure. It's only half an hour till I make my stage debut.

(Harvard exits.)

LINDA: The trick to landing your man is feeling confident. I've got something that will help.

(Linda produces a 1950s cone-style bra.)

MEI-LI: Oh, no—I couldn't!
LINDA: Wearing one of these is like driving a big ol' Cadillac. Anyone gets in your way, you just mow 'em right down.

(Harvard and four Showgirls return with the dress.)

HARVARD: Voilà!
LINDA: And if this doesn't close the deal with Ta, I'll take vows as a nun.
MEI-LI: It looks like something out of a Hollywood movie.
LINDA: Try it on.
MEI-LI: Here, now?
HARVARD: Honey, these girls take off their clothes three times a night for total strangers.

(Mei-li, Harvard and the Showgirls go upstage behind a screen.)

LINDA: And whatever you got, he's seen plenty of times before.
HARVARD: In all shapes and sizes.
SHOWGIRL 1: Who's the lucky guy?
SHOWGIRL 2: You have a nice little figure, young lady.

SHOWGIRL 3: Yeah!

SHOWGIRL 4: You ought to show it off more.

LINDA: She will. This is just the beginning.

MEI-LI: In China, a woman is only considered beautiful if she remains so into old age.

LINDA: So what—you've gotta wait 'til you're sixty to get a date? This is the land of fast food, fast cars—

(Mei-li emerges from behind the screen. She looks beautiful in Linda's dress.)

—and overnight sensations.

(A Stage Manager enters.)

STAGE MANAGER: Come on, ladies—I called "places" five minutes ago! We've got three shows tonight! Let's go!

(Stage Manager, Harvard and the Showgirls exit.)

MEI-LI: I don't know how to thank you.

LINDA: Once you've landed Ta, the two of you can think of something sentimental: like ten percent of the gate.

(Linda exits, leaving Mei-li at the dressing room mirror. She studies her reflection.
Song—"I Enjoy Being a Girl [Reprise]":)

MEI-LI:

> I'm strictly a female female,
> And my future, I hope, will be—

(Linda and Ta meet backstage, unseen by Mei-li.)

TA *(To Linda)*: A kiss? For good luck?

LINDA: You know, Ta, when you made me wear that Chinese robe—you were right. You've been right about a lot of things. After the show, I promise you a big surprise— that'll make tonight even more special.

(Linda kisses Ta, then exits. Ta follows her, stars in his eyes. Mei-li remains at the dressing room table, unaware of their exchange.)

MEI-LI:
> In the home of a brave and free male
> Who'll enjoy being a guy
> Having a girl like me.

SCENE 8

Onstage and backstage at the theatre. Ta serves as emcee at the microphone.

TA: Honorable ladies and gentlemen: welcome to the grand opening of the jewel of the New Chinatown—Club Chop Suey!

*(Linda enters.
Song—"Fan Tan Fannie":)*

LINDA:
> Fan Tan Fannie
> Was leaving her man,
> Fan Tan Fannie
> Kept waving her fan,
> Said "Good-bye Danny
> You two-timing Dan,
> Some other man
> Loves your little Fannie!
> Bye, bye!

In the ice-box
You'll find in a can,
Some left-overs
Of Moo-Goo-Guy-Pan.
Fan Tan Fannie
Has found a new guy,
His name is Manny,
He's good for Fannie,
So good-bye Danny,
Good-bye!"

(Chorus Boys and Showgirls enter, dance with Linda. Backstage. Liang and Wang watch from the wings.)

WANG: This is disgusting! They're having the time of their lives!
LIANG: Remind you a little of your own audiences? Back in China?
WANG: There is no comparison! This mob has come only to have a good time. In China, none of my audiences ever expected to have a good time! I have half a mind to toss them all out of here. This is no longer my theatre.

(Wang starts to leave. Chin enters.)

CHIN: Master Wang—I have heard that the mayor himself may pay a visit.

(Wang stops in his tracks, impressed despite himself.)

WANG: The mayor? In *my* theatre?

(Back to the onstage performance.)

LINDA AND COMPANY:
"Fan Tan Fannie
Has found a new guy,

His name is Manny,
He's good for Fannie,
So good-bye Danny,
Good-bye!
... Bye bye!
... Bye bye!
Hope you like Moo-Goo-Guy-Pan!"

(The number ends. Linda and the Showgirls perform a "playoff," singing and dancing a brief coda to the number, as they exit the nightclub stage.)

LINDA AND SHOWGIRLS:
  "Bye! Bye!
  Bye! Bye!"

LINDA:
  "Ciao, ciao Danny,"

LINDA AND SHOWGIRLS:
  "Good-bye!
  Bye! Bye!"

(Backstage, Ta calls "places" for the next number.)

TA: Places for "Vagabond Sailor"! Places, please!

(Onstage, Harvard enters in a sailor's suit and begins to perform "Vagabond Sailor":)

HARVARD:
  I am a vagabond sailor ...

(Back to Liang and Wang, backstage.)

LIANG: There's a line outside stretching half-way down the block.

WANG: This sort of work—it requires no talent. Anyone can do it.

LIANG: Oh, I know you're above all this, Chi-Yang. Playing before packed houses, feeling the love and adoration? It's not the sort of thing any actor really wants.

(Chin enters.)

CHIN: And we're expecting a larger house for the second show!

(Jump forward in time to the second Club Chop Suey show. Linda and the Showgirls are once again onstage, performing the "playoff" to "Fan Tan Fannie":)

LINDA AND SHOWGIRLS:
      ". . . Bye! Bye!
      Bye! Bye!"

LINDA:
      "Ciao, ciao Danny,"

LINDA AND SHOWGIRLS:
      "Good-bye!
      Bye! Bye!"

(Backstage, Ta calls places for the next number.)

TA: Places for "Vagabond Sailor"! Places, please!

(In his sailor's costume, Harvard enters onstage to perform "Vagabond Sailor":)

HARVARD:
> I am a vagabond sailor . . .

(Back to Wang and Liang, backstage.)

WANG: Madame Liang, can I have a word with you? About that boy onstage?

LIANG: Harvard?

WANG: I've been watching him practice all week. Couldn't you find anyone more convincing to play a sailor?

LIANG: Well, in exchange for a featured spot, he made all the costumes for free.

WANG: Where is your integrity? That number is never going to work until you put the right actor into the part.

(Chin enters.)

CHIN: It's confirmed! The mayor's coming to the third show!

(Jump forward in time to the third show. Linda and the Showgirls perform the "playoff" to "Fan Tan Fannie":)

LINDA AND SHOWGIRLS:
> ". . . Bye! Bye!
> Bye! Bye!"

LINDA:
> "Ciao, ciao Danny,"

LINDA AND SHOWGIRLS:
> "Good-bye!
> Bye! Bye!"

(Backstage, Ta calls places for the next number.)

TA: Places for "Vagabond Sailor"! Places, please!

(Backstage, Harvard enters in his underwear.)

HARVARD: Madame Liang! Madame Liang, I can't find my costume! I can't find my costume!

(Onstage, Wang enters. A spotlight hits him standing stiffly in Harvard's sailor suit.
Song—"Gliding Through My Memoree":)

WANG:

> I am a vagabond sailor . . .
> All my friends call me sport—
> I am a fellow for action,
> Any storm in a port—
>
> Now that I'm home and I'm resting,

(The Sailor's Quartet enters onstage, and are surprised to see that Wang has taken Harvard's place.)

> Home from over the sea,
> All of the girls who adored me
> Go gliding through my memoree!

(The Showgirls come out in costumes denoting different countries. As he interacts with them, Wang begins to loosen up, his stage instincts taking over until he's hamming it up, having the time of his life.)

> A sweet colleen from Ireland,
> Her hair was fiery red,
> Her eyes gave out a green light
> That said I could go ahead.

I met a girl in Sweden
Of whom I grew quite fond,
A stately Scandinavian type,
A buxom, blue-eyed blonde—

(Ad-libbing, regarding the "Swedish girl":)

Now, *that's* my idea of Chinese take-out.

And then, in merry England,
A girl who worshipped me,
Gliding through my memoree—
That's how I see them,
Gliding through my memoree!

SAILOR'S QUARTET:
 Hey, sport, there are many more girls

WANG:
 In sunny Barcelona,
 A dancing chick I picked.
 Her castanets were clicking
 Like nothing ever clicked!

SAILOR'S QUARTET:
 Ole!
 A very friendly ma'amselle in oo-la-la-Paree,

FRENCH GIRL:
 Oo-la-la!

WANG:
 She was a girl who couldn't say anything but

FRENCH GIRL:
    Oui!

WANG AND SAILOR'S QUARTET:
    'Twas fun to cast an anchor
    In lovely Casablanker.
    I loved a Grecian doll and
    Another doll in Holland,
    But of all the girls in every hemisphere,
    There is no one like the girl I have right here—
    Right here on . . .

(Linda enters, costumed as Miss Grant Avenue.)

ALL:
    Grant Avenue,
    San Francisco,
    California,
    U.S.A.

WANG:
    Yes, Grant Avenue
    Where is that?

ALL:
    San Francisco,
    That's where's that!
    California,
    U.
    S.
    A . . .

(Curtain drops.)

SCENE 9

Backstage, Liang, Chin and Ta run on to join the company and congratulate Wang.

LIANG: You were wonderful!

WANG: Now we have shown them the New Chinatown!

HARVARD: You stole my costume!

WANG: That was wrong, I know. But the first job of any actor is to find a way to get onstage!

LIANG: Wasn't that more satisfying than the opera?

WANG: Of course not! But it was a lot more fun. Listen everyone—after you get out of your costumes, we will meet in one of those evil dance halls—and celebrate until dawn! Drinks are on me!

(Company members cheer, then begin to exit as the set is struck.)

LINDA: Careful, Ta. Next thing you know, Uncle Wang's gonna want to restage all your numbers!

WANG: Uncle Wang. Maybe I need a stage name. Who is that *American* uncle? The wise sage with the pointed finger and the white beard?

LIANG: You want people to call you "Uncle Sam"?

WANG: How about "Uncle Sammy"?

CHIN: "Sammy Wong"!

LIANG: "Sammy *Fong*"!

WANG: Yes—from now on, I shall be known as "Uncle Sammy Fong"!

LIANG *(To company)*: Come on, troops. Let's get you ready for the cameras.

WANG *(To Chin)*: Just like the old days, huh?

CHIN: Not exactly.

(The remaining company members and Chin exit, leaving Ta and Wang alone.)

TA: Dad, this was *my* club. I can't believe that on my opening night, you actually had the nerve to go out there and—and—

WANG: And make that number work? Son, we're a team. It was watching *you* these past weeks that inspired me—to think I could learn this new style, too.

(Pause.)

You're not angry with me, are you?

TA: I guess . . . you can't argue with success.

WANG: Why did it take me so long to understand? That all this time, you were actually making this club—to be my destiny.

TA: Um, that's one way of looking at it.

WANG: You are the most filial son on this continent! If our ancestors could see us now, I'll bet they would just die!

(Wang exits. Harvard crosses the stage.)

HARVARD: Now who's the wise guy that took my street clothes?

(Stage Manager enters.)

TA: You know where Linda is?

STAGE MANAGER: Last time I saw her, she was backstage changing.

TA: She says she has a big surprise for me.

STAGE MANAGER: Sure she does, Ta. Everyone loves a winner.

(Stage Manager exits. Linda enters, in a glittering, sexy opening-night dress. Ta sees her.)

TA: Hey! So where are we going? Top of the Mark? The Coconut Grove?

LINDA: Right idea, wrong girl.

TA: But you said—?

LINDA: Uh-huh. And wait 'til you see her. She's all grown-up.

(Mei-li enters, wearing Linda's yellow dress from earlier.)

MEI-LI: Hello, Ta.

TA *(To Linda)*: Wait—you meant . . . ? This was your idea of a big surprise? To stick Mei-li into one of your old dresses?

MEI-LI: We thought . . . you'd like it.

TA: "*We* thought." So lemme get this straight. The two of you— what?—made a deal? *(To Mei-li)* I'd date *you (To Linda)* to get *you* off the hook? How long has this been going on?

LINDA: I was just trying to help you both.

TA: How? By presenting her to me like a, a consolation prize? *(Pause; to Mei-li)* I'm sorry, I didn't mean—

LINDA: No, you just can't help ruining a good thing for yourself. *(To Mei-li)* I'm sorry, honey. I thought he was smarter than that.

(Linda exits.)

TA: Mei-li, don't get me wrong. You're a great kid, but—

MEI-LI: —but I should never have put on this dress.

TA: You look beautiful. It's not the dress.

MEI-LI: Then it's me you don't want, isn't it? Someone fresh off the boat, who doesn't know how to dress, or wear her hair—

TA: I—

MEI-LI: You're right, Ta, I don't fit in here. I'm just some foolish refugee—who thought you kissed me . . . because you loved me.

(Mei-li runs offstage, as Wang enters in a Western-style suit.)

WANG: Son, some American movie star has asked us to dinner. I have never heard of her, so she must be very popular.

(Liang enters.)

LIANG *(To Ta)*: Doesn't your father look handsome in his new suit?

WANG: You think so? American clothes pinch in the strangest places.

TA: Sorry, I've gotta clean up this big mess I've made.

LIANG: Where are you going? You're a star now, not the janitor.

TA: You don't understand, this is important.

(Linda enters.)

LINDA: It could've been important. But now it's too late. Nice going, Ta.

LIANG: I don't know what's going on between the two of you, but our Hollywood friends are waiting. Listen, an opportunity like this only comes around once in a lifetime. And for a Chinese person, it's probably never happened—ever.

WANG: Son?

TA: I guess the other thing can wait.

LIANG: Of course it can. All right, let's make an exit!

(They walk outside and are greeted by photographers and reporters. After a beat, Mei-li enters, followed by Chin. She has changed back into the clothes she wore upon arriving in America.)

CHIN: Mei-li, what happened to your dress?

MEI-LI: It was not my dress. And it never will be. I guess kissing means nothing in this country. Does *anything* mean something around here?

CHIN: Even when times were hard, your father never stopped believing that miracles can happen.

MEI-LI: My father is dead, Uncle Chin. So don't talk to me about miracles. Maybe they happen sometimes, for some people. But not for me.

CHIN: So you're leaving? But where will you go?

MEI-LI: All I know is that I can't stay at the club. I'll start over again—some way, somehow.

(Chin exits.
Song—"A Hundred Million Miracles [Reprise]":)

A hundred million miracles—
What a foolish thing to say.
Who expects a miracle
To happen every day?

(Mei-li steps out into the streets of Chinatown, where she rejoins groups of New Immigrants. The once-bright city now looks bleak and forbidding to them.)

My father says
That children keep growing,
Rivers keep flowing, too.
My father says
He doesn't know why
But, somehow or other . . .

ENSEMBLE *(Echoing Mei-li):*
Somehow or other . . .

MEI-LI:
>   Somehow or other . . .

(Carrying her drum in its satchel, Mei-li joins the other Immigrants to face the challenges of their new lives in Chinatown.
>   *Curtain. End of Act One.)*

ACT TWO

SCENE 1

Onstage at the very flashy Club Chop Suey, several months later. Reflecting their new-found prosperity, the theatre now features neon, smoke and over-the-top "Oriental" motifs.

Wang in his stage persona of Sammy Fong is discovered in a giant take-out container. He is dressed as a chef, and backed-up by Chorus Boys who dance with giant chopsticks.

Song—"Chop Suey":)

WANG:

> Chop suey!
> Chop suey!
> Good and bad, intelligent, mad and screwy,
>
> Violins and trumpets and drums—
> Take it all the way that it comes.
> Sad and funny, sour and honeydewy—
>
> Chop suey!

CHORUS BOYS:
> Chop suey . . .

WANG *(To audience)*: Welcome to Club Chop Suey where East meets West seven swinging nights a week. Tonight Sammy has prepared for your pleasure, Ancient Chinese Delicacy!

WANG AND CHORUS BOYS:
> Chop suey . . .

(The Showgirls enter wearing giant take-out containers which light-up from within.)

CHORUS BOYS:
> Chop suey . . .
> Chop suey . . .
> Chop suey!

WANG: Here at Uncle Sammy's we offer you one from column A. Or . . . you could choose . . . one from column B. And don't forget MSG. For more—stunning—girls . . .
SHOWGIRLS: We deliver!

(The Showgirls in their take-out boxes dance with the Chorus Boys carrying their chopsticks.)

CHORUS BOYS:
> Chop suey! . . . Suey! . . . Suey!

WANG: Feeling hungry yet?

ENSEMBLE:
> Aaai-ya!

WANG: I know I am! And I just ate an hour ago. Some of you may be wondering, What are those long wooden things on my plate? These are called chopsticks . . .

ENSEMBLE:

>Chop-chop-chop-chew-wah!

WANG: . . . and they're so much fun to use.

ENSEMBLE:

>Chop-chop-chop-chew-wah!

WANG: Just grab a pair . . .

ENSEMBLE:

>Chop-chop

WANG *(Spoken)*: . . . squeeze, lift to your mouth and

ENSEMBLE *(Singing)*: Chop-chop-chop and

ALL:

>Ooo-eee!

ENSEMBLE:

>Chop suey . . .

WANG: Can you dig it?
ENSEMBLE: All the way to China!

>*(The music to "Chop Suey" continues to play, the ensemble continues to dance, as we go with Wang backstage to his dressing room. He starts to change into his next costume. Liang enters and knocks on the dressing room door.)*

LIANG:

>Chop suey!

>*(Spoken)* $2,572.29!

(They both scream with excitement.)

WANG: Just a few months ago, I was playing to empty houses!
LIANG: Sammy, with my management skills, and your need to be loved, we can't lose.

ENSEMBLE:
Chop suey!

WANG: Americans are such warm and loving people.
LIANG: But what we really want from them is respect. And nothing in this country buys respect like money.

ENSEMBLE:
Chop suey!

(Ta enters Wang's dressing room.)

WANG: Son, have you thought about our new idea?
TA: The "Swinging Confucius" number?
WANG: I come out as: Master Confucius, Ancient Oriental Wiseguy.
TA: You guys ever think we might be going just a bit too far?
WANG *(As Confucius)*: Confucius say, "Two whites don't make a Wong." *(As himself)* What do you mean, "too far?"
TA: What happened to the "New Chinatown"?
LIANG: Sure, we'll give the tourists what they want, but we'll have the last laugh.
TA: You don't care that you're making us look ridiculous?
WANG: Sammy Fong is not ridiculous!
TA: No? Has Sammy looked in the mirror lately?
WANG: All the time. And whenever I do, I thank Sammy Fong. Because without him, I would turn back into just another Chinaman. And so would you.

SHOWGIRLS:
> Chop suey,
> Chop suey
> Living here is very much like
> Chop suey!

(Linda, wearing her "I Enjoy Being a Girl" costume, enters Wang's dressing room.)

LINDA: What's this about working Uncle Sammy into my "Fresh Off the Boat" number?
WANG: We thought the number could use some jokes.
LINDA: Like all my other dances? *(Pulls out the long sleeves of her Chinese robe)* Careful, these could wind up 'round someone's neck. *(To Liang)* Some agent you turned out to be.

(Linda exits.)

LIANG: Hey, you're working, aren't you?
WANG *(Off, to Linda)*: Confucius say, "Girl whose head gets too big may end up falling on face!"
TA: I'll calm her down. And Dad, stop with the Confucius jokes, all right?

(Ta exits.)

WANG: That kid. What does he want from me?
LIANG: Don't worry about Ta. Here's *my* New Deal: a Chinatown in every city, and a Club Chop Suey in every Chinatown.

WANG *(Sings)*:
> Boston, Austin, Wichita and St. Louis—

LIANG:

> Chop suey!

WANG: And we will serve Chinese food along with their local delicacies! *(Sings:)*

> Peking Duck and Mulligan stew,

LIANG:

> Plymouth Rock and Little Rock, too.

WANG:

> Milk and beer and Seven-Up and Drambuie—

WANG AND LIANG:

> Chop suey!

(Harvard enters with Wang's outfit for the next number: an Uncle Sam costume.)

HARVARD: You're on, Lady Liberty.

(Harvard helps Wang dress.)

WANG *(To Liang)*: After the show tonight, how 'bout we celebrate with a drink at the Coconut Grove.

LIANG: Sammy! I thought you didn't like to spend good money just to get drunk?

WANG: I don't. But it's time to start living the good life—whether I like it or not.

(Liang exits, followed by Harvard. Wang stands in his Uncle Sam costume. The Showgirls in their take-out container outfits, images of his mind, surround him in his dressing room.)

WANG (*Looking upward*): My dear wife in heaven: it didn't turn out quite like we'd planned, did it? You know how hard I tried. But I couldn't get them to love our opera here—I couldn't even convince our own son. And you know how much I love the sound of an audience. So can you please forgive me, that I have finally begun to find happiness? (*Sings:*)

>   Chop suey . . .

SHOWGIRLS:
>   Chop-chop-chop

WANG:
>   Chop suey . . .

SHOWGIRLS:
>   Chop-chop-chop

WANG:
>   Chop suey . . .

SHOWGIRLS:
>   Chop-chop-chop

WANG:
>   Chop suey . . .

SHOWGIRLS:
>   Chop-chop-chop

WANG AND SHOWGIRLS:
>   Chop suey . . .
>   Chop-chop-chop-chew-wah!

(Wang exits to the stage, to resume his new role as Uncle Sammy.)

SCENE 2

The theatre, later that night. Ta enters, still upset from his last exchange with his father. Looking around the empty stage, he begins to hear the music from "You Are Beautiful." Remembering his Chinese opera dance with Mei-li, he starts to perform the male role by himself. Upstage, a vision of Mei-li appears where the Ghost Couple had danced before. He watches her until she disappears. Unseen by Ta, Chin enters and observes him.

CHIN: The things we learn when we are young, we can never really forget.

TA *(Startled)*: Uncle Chin! You're still here?

CHIN: If only your father had allowed you to play the male roles. I always knew you would be magnificent.

TA: So how do *you* feel? About all the changes around here?

CHIN: I make more money now as a janitor than I ever did in the opera.

TA: I'm amazed you've still stuck around. Sometimes I think we're turning into some kind of weird Oriental minstrel show.

CHIN: But this club has given Chi-Yang something very rare: a second chance at his life. He's become more like the man he used to be. Of course, he used to have better taste.

TA: And it's all my fault.

CHIN: Then you should be proud of yourself.

TA: How can one man change so much? What's happening to him?

CHIN: What do you think? He's finally starting to let go . . . of the memory of your mother.

TA: I wish I'd been old enough to really see them together. Mei-li was starting to tell me what she knew, but . . .

CHIN: Still looking for her?

TA: I've tried everything, with no luck.

CHIN: If you found Mei-li, what would you say?

TA: First, that I am so sorry for the way I treated her.

CHIN: And that you love her?

TA: I'm in love with someone else.

CHIN: Linda? Why? Because you want to prove that you're good enough for her?

TA: What makes you think that?

CHIN: They don't call me "Big-Ear Chin" for nothing.

TA: How would you understand, Uncle Chin? You've been married to the same woman your entire life.

CHIN: So I obviously know nothing about love. The best wisdom I ever received about love was given to me by Chi-Yang's father.

TA: My grandfather?

CHIN: He took me in, after my own parents died. That is why I "stick around," Ta. Because I was once as young as you. And before that, even younger.

(Song—"My Best Love":)

How can a young man know where his heart will go?
Only an old man knows what a man should know.
All that was true for me shall be true for you.
You are romantic, I was romantic, too.

A new true love I'd meet each day,
The girls were fresh and sweet,
Like buds in May.
Like buds that grew in May,
They bloomed and blew away.

73

Then I met my young bride-to-be,
Radiant and lovely was she.
When all the other loves had passed,
My best love came last.

TA: So what's your secret for a long and happy marriage?
CHIN: For one thing, I am hardly ever at home. But whenever I return, it is as if we were never apart.
TA: This is pointless. I can't even find Mei-li.
CHIN: She is working at the On Leock Fortune Cookie Company. On Stockton St.
TA: You knew? And you haven't told me?
CHIN: She made me promise not to. But I am an old man. And I sometimes forget what I promised. Ta, think about yourself a little less—and Mei-li a little more. Then you may start to become the man you see in her eyes. Now go!

(Ta exits. Chin sings:)

All that was true for me shall be true for you.
You are romantic, I was romantic, too.

SCENE 3

The On Leock Fortune Cookie Factory. Factory Workers, including Mei-li and Chao, enter. They sing an ironic reprise of "I Am Going to Like It Here":

FACTORY WORKERS:
I am going to like it here.
There is something about the place,
An encouraging atmosphere,
Like a smile on a friendly face.

There is something about the place,
So caressing and warm it is—
Like a smile on a friendly face,
Like a port in a storm it is!

(As the Workers arrive, Mr. Chong, the factory owner, checks them in for the day.)

So caressing and warm it is—
All the people are so sincere—
Like a port in a storm it is!

(Chong claps, signaling the beginning of the work day.)

I am going to like it . . .

(As Chong exits and the Workers move into place, Chao crosses to Mei-li.)

CHAO: When the boss wasn't looking, I slipped some of my own fortunes into the cookies.
MEI-LI: Chao!
CHAO: You think any restaurant is gonna order more cookies that read, "Stop eating now, you're already too darn fat"?
MEI-LI *(Laughs)*: You could lose your job!
CHAO: Big deal. So long as I make you smile.

(He tries to kiss her. She moves away.)

MEI-LI: Chao, we're only friends.
CHAO: I know, a classy girl like you doesn't fall in love with peasant stock overnight.
MEI-LI: That's not it.

(She joins the other Workers on the line.)

CHAO: But I can help you, Mei-li. If you just let me take you away from here.

MEI-LI: I can't believe you're really thinking about—

CHAO: Hong Kong. That is where we belong.

MEI-LI: We haven't even been in this country a year.

CHAO: Look at the Chinese here—waiters, cooks, laundrymen.

MEI-LI: I've met some successful Chinese.

CHAO: They live a little better than we do. And try so hard to fit in, they don't even know who they are no more. I'm a practical man. And it's never gonna happen for me over here.

(Ta enters, sees Mei-li.)

TA: Mei-li.

MEI-LI: Ta?

TA: I've been looking everywhere for you.

CHAO: Speak of the white devil.

TA *(To Chao)*: Hey, I'm Chinese, too. *(To Mei-li)* One hundred percent, remember?

(Chong enters.)

CHONG: Chao—delivery!

CHAO: But you don't like it, do you?

(Chao crosses to Chong. They exit together.)

TA *(To Mei-li)*: I guess I deserved that.

MEI-LI: Please leave me alone. Before I lose my job.

(Chong reenters, sees Ta.)

CHONG: Wang Ta? The Prince of Chinatown?

(Chong shakes Ta's hand.)

TA: I need to speak with her for a few minutes.
CHONG: Go ahead! I love your father, he's so funny!

(Chong exits.)

TA: Mei-li, I want to apologize for that night. I was stupid—
and wrong.
MEI-LI: If you have anything to be sorry about, it's that you
kissed me in the first place.
TA: I'm not sorry about that.
MEI-LI: Why? Because kissing means nothing to you?
TA: No, because kissing *you* meant a lot to me.
MEI-LI: Ta, I don't know what you want—and neither do you.
TA: I want you to come back to the club. When I was around
you, I felt proud to be me—for the first time in my life.
I need you, Mei-li.
MEI-LI: More than you need Linda?

(Pause.)

I don't want to be your second choice. Especially now,
when I know how it feels to have a man want me—the way
you want Linda.
TA: You mean . . . that guy? The two of you aren't—together,
are you?
MEI-LI: What if we are?
TA: He's never gonna get you out of Chinatown. He's too old-
fashioned, he doesn't know the customs here, and he's
always going to make you feel like a foreigner.
MEI-LI: Aren't all those things also true—about me?

TA: No! I didn't mean—

MEI-LI: I can't go back to the club. Maybe I make you feel proud to be you, Ta. But you always make me feel . . . ashamed to be me.

(Chao enters.)

That's why Chao and I have decided to try our luck in Hong Kong.

TA: What?

CHAO: The place is gonna be big someday—put all those Chinese together, give them a chance to make money— how can they go wrong?

TA: You can't go back there!

CHAO: Maybe *you* can't. You hardly speak the language.

TA: Someone does not cross the Pacific in the bottom of a freighter just to turn and head back to Hong Kong.

MEI-LI: Ta, one of these fortunes has always reminded me of you *(She hands him a fortune)*

TA *(Reading)*: "A man cannot love others until he learns to love himself."

MEI-LI: So—will you please wish us well?

CHAO *(To Ta)*: No hard feelings?

TA: No hard feelings. Mei-li, I hope you're happy. I really do.

(Ta exits.)

CHAO *(To Mei-li)*: Did you mean it?

(Mei-li nods.)

Let's celebrate with a big dinner: fish heads and chicken feet?

MEI-LI: Who could resist?

CHONG (*Entering*): Chao!

> (*Chao talks with Chong. Mei-li removes her drum from its satchel. Chong exits, and Chao returns to Mei-li.*)

CHAO (*Referring to the drum*): What's that? You look like a little girl, with your dolly.
MEI-LI: This has been in my family for—for many years.

> (*He takes the drum, examines it.*)

CHAO: The Americans, they can't tell a beggar's drum from a fancy antique. If we sell this—we can raise money for the trip.

> (*Pause.*)

Unless . . . it's so important to you.
MEI-LI: I guess—I don't need it any longer.
CHAO: Thank you. Your life is going to be good now, just leave everything to me.

> (*Chao exits with the drum. "I Am Going to Like It Here" underscores Mei-li's exit with her empty satchel.*)

SCENE 4

Golden Dragon Restaurant. Wang and Liang enter. The owner, Mr. Lee, welcomes them.

LIANG: Table for two.
LEE: Sammy? Sammy Fong—is that you?
WANG: Sssh. Call me Chi-Yang. Tonight, I am seeking privacy.
LEE: I am so honored that you return to my humble establishment.

LIANG: He needed some soul food.

(Lee seats them, hands them menus.)

LEE: Tonight's specials.
LIANG: You decide, but we just want a little snack.
LEE: Of course. Cocktails on the house.

(Lee takes two drinks from a waitress, leaves them, and then exits.)

WANG: Unbelievable!
LIANG: Now, Sammy—think about your blood pressure.
WANG: Was that a crime? To show Ta a number I'd staged on my own? Suddenly, he throws a fit and storms out of the nightclub. You know what that boy's problem is? He needs a girlfriend.
LIANG: I heard that opera girl liked him.
WANG: Mei-li? They would have been perfect together.
LIANG: That's what happens once you have some success in show biz—suddenly, your love life goes down the drain.
WANG: Mine's been down there for years—even when I was a failure. How did you learn so much about show business, anyway?
LIANG: I was once a starlet.
WANG: Really?
LIANG: Down in Hollywood. They called me "The Queen of the Oriental Crowd Scenes." Whenever a Japanese village got bombed, that was me, screaming. But glory like that can't last. One day, your looks fade, you gain a few pounds, some new girl comes along who can shriek a little louder. And you're left bitter, barely educated, with no useful skills. What could I do? I became an agent.
WANG: Madame Liang, I would never say that your looks have faded.

LIANG: You can call me Rita.

WANG: If only we had met years ago—Rita. Look how you make me bend to your every desire. And, yet, I am so happy!

LIANG: And what if I wanted you to marry me?

WANG: But you're already married, aren't you?

LIANG: Whatever gave you that idea?

WANG: Then why do you call yourself *Madame* Liang?

LIANG: I *was* married. But I got over it. You mean, you thought—?

WANG: Forgive me!

LIANG: Sammy, I'm going to save you a lot of pain: I am the world's worst wife. If you don't believe me, check the court record.

WANG: You are divorced?

LIANG: Four times. Can that many ex-husbands be wrong? Under oath?

WANG: I'm worse. I expect a wife to walk three paces behind me. Except when we step into traffic.

LIANG: Anyway, you want a young lotus blossom, not an old lotus root.

WANG: Look at me—I'm practically fermented!

LIANG: Don't gimme that.

(Song—"Don't Marry Me":)

> You are young and beautiful,
> Sweet as the breath of May.
> Earnestly I speak to you—
> Weigh every word I say:
>
> If you want to have a rosy future
> And be happy as a honey bee,
> With a missus who will always love you, baby,
> Don't marry me!

WANG:

> If you want a man you can depend on,
> I can absolutely guarantee
> I will never fail to disappoint you, baby,
> Don't marry me!
>
> I eat litchi nuts and cookies in bed,
> And I fill the bed with nutshells and crumbs.

LIANG:

> I have irritating habits you'll dread,
> Like the way I have of cracking my thumbs!
>
> My grandpa was a big game hunter,
> He met grandma swinging on a tree—
> If you want to have attractive children, baby,
> Don't marry me!

(Food is served.)

> I'm devoted to my dear old mama

WANG:

> And if me and mama disagree,

LIANG:

> I would always side with her against you, schnookie,

WANG:

> Don't marry me.
>
> I would always like to know where you go.
> I don't like a wife to keep me in doubt—

LIANG:

> Honey, that's a thing that's easy to know—
> You will always know where *I* am, I'm out!
>
> I am talking like a Chinese uncle,

WANG:

> I am serious as I can be,

LIANG:

> I am saying this because I love you,

WANG:

> darling,

LIANG AND WANG:

> Don't marry me!

(Dishes are cleared, as Liang and Wang read their fortunes.)

LIANG:

> Marry a dope,
> Innocent and gaga.

WANG:

> Marry a Khan—
> Ali or the Aga.

LIANG:

> Marry for money

WANG:

> Or marry for free,

LIANG AND WANG:

> BUT DON'T MARRY ME!

(Liang pays the bill and they leave the restaurant.)

WANG: See you at the club tomorrow?

LIANG: Tomorrow's our day off, silly. Aren't you looking forward to it?

WANG *(After a pause)*: No.

LIANG: Oh, Sammy—that's the nicest thing any man's said to me in years.

WANG *(Sings)*:
    I am saying this because I love you,

LIANG:
    darling . . .

(They kiss, then exit.)

SCENE 5

Weeks later. The stage. Linda enters, with Harvard behind her, carrying suitcases.

HARVARD: You can't do this to me!

LINDA: Harvard, this isn't about you.

HARVARD: From my perspective, *everything's* about me!

LINDA: I've gotten an offer from an agent in L.A., and I'm going to accept.

HARVARD: Say it ain't so, Low!

LINDA: Uncle Sammy's made himself the star of this show. Before you know it, he'll be doing the stripping, too. You should've seen this coming the night he first stole your costume.

HARVARD: You're right, but I've come to think of these people as my family. So I expect them to treat me like dirt.

LINDA: Things going any better with your real parents?

HARVARD *(With accent, mimicking his parents)*: "We are *so* disappointed in you!" *(Himself again)* I've decided it's a genetic problem. They're Chinese, and I'm not a doctor. Think about it: these are the same two people who named me "Harvard."

LINDA: To me, you'll always be ivy league. Now let's get out of here before I run into anyone.

HARVARD: You go down there and you make it, OK? For *us*.

(Ta enters.)

TA: Linda, there you are!

LINDA: Oh god.

HARVARD: I guess you two young people would like some time alone. *(To Linda)* He made you a star. Now, at least say good-bye.

(Harvard exits.)

LINDA: Ta, I just came to pack my things, I'm not in the mood for a big—

TA: I think what you're doing is great.

LINDA: You do?

TA: I mean, most of us don't have the courage. But you—you're actually going to make a go of it.

LINDA: Well . . . thank you, Ta.

TA: I'm going to Hollywood, too.

LINDA: Now wait a minute.

TA: I think we're a good team. In L.A., we could put together an act for casting agents.

LINDA: I can't believe this.

TA: Maybe even start our own theatre—you know, on their home turf!

LINDA: Ta, you are not the kind of guy who'd walk away from your own father's nightclub!

TA: What makes you so sure?

LINDA: Because you're a good Chinese son!

TA: From the day we first met, all I have ever done is try to give you whatever you want.

LINDA: And you expect me to love you for that? I'm sorry. I can't.

TA: What's wrong with me? Am I ugly or something?

LINDA: Of course not.

TA: Am I stupid? Or mean?

LINDA: I'm not in love with you, it's that simple.

TA: Because I'm Chinese?

LINDA: I've gotta go.

TA: Funny thing about your boyfriends: they all look alike.

LINDA: I'm not gonna get into this.

TA: How come you only date white guys, anyway?

LINDA: How come? For the same reason you always hated doing Chinese opera. We all wanna be Americans—like everyone else.

(Pause.)

When I'm out with my boyfriends, no one ever says to me, "Go back to where you came from." Is that so terrible? To feel now and then like I actually belong here?

TA: So that's all love means to you? A chance to grab another status symbol?

LINDA: You should understand. Aren't you the guy that doesn't date anyone who's fresh off the boat?

TA: That's completely different!

LINDA: C'mon, Ta—deep down, you and I are too much alike, maybe that's our problem.

TA: What do you mean?

LINDA: Neither one of us wants to love someone who reminds us too much of ourselves. So . . . good luck to us both.

TA: Linda, don't you get it? I've got no other place to go! You're my first love . . . and my last chance.

LINDA: Look, I'm leaving on the seven A.M. Greyhound. If you wanna come along, it's your choice. I'm not responsible.

TA: I've got no other choices. Dad's taken over the club, and Mei-li's headed for Hong Kong.

LINDA: Guess that explains why I saw her drum hanging in the pawn shop on Kearny Street.

TA: Her flower drum? Are you sure?

LINDA: I thought that thing was important to her, too.

TA: She can't give it up now.

LINDA: Sure she can. People losing hope, giving up their dreams—it happens every day.

(Linda exits, Ta follows, as we transition into:)

SCENE 6

The docks. Emigrants enter, packed to leave America, returning home.

EMIGRANTS *(Singing)*:
California,
U.S.A.

EMIGRANT #1: I was so lonely, no one spoke my dialect, I could not stand it any longer! I have to go home.

EMIGRANT #2: Can someone take my child back to Hong Kong? I can not make enough to support us both. I will send for him one day, I promise.

EMIGRANT #3: I am a physicist! And they made me scrub floors, like a coolie!

EMIGRANT #4: Every word he ever spoke to me was a lie. He told me to come, and be his wife. He promised to make all my wishes come true.

(Mei-li, among the Emigrants, is also ready to leave the country.
Song—"Love, Look Away":)

MEI-LI:
I have wished before.
I will wish no more.

Love, look away!
Love, look away from me.
Fly, when you pass my door,
Fly and get lost at sea.
Call it a day.
Love, let us say we're through,
No good are you for me,
No good am I for you.

Wanting you so, I try too much.
After you go, I cry too much.

Love, look away.
Lonely though I may be,
Leave me and set me free,
Look away, look away, look away from me.

(Chao enters, carrying their bags.)

CHAO: I paid that guy good money to get us on the ship, where is he? *(He sees Mei-li's sadness)* What's wrong? Mei-li, I promise I'll make you happy.
MEI-LI: Then kiss me.
CHAO: Now? But I still got to find—
MEI-LI: Just kiss me.

(He does, without much passion. A boat whistles.)

CHAO: I'm sorry. I got to get us on that boat—or nothing else matters.

(Chao exits.)

MEI-LI:
      Wanting you so, I try too much.
      After you go, I cry too much.

      Love, look away.
      Lonely though I may be,
      Leave me and set me free,
      Look away, look away, look away from me.

(Chao enters.)

CHAO: I found him, everything's fine. Now I give you a real kiss.

(Ta enters.)

TA: I didn't come to cause trouble. Mei-li, I just don't think you should leave without this.

(He produces her flower drum.)

CHAO: You actually bought that thing? Do you see? Americans cannot tell the difference.
TA: I may not know as much about China as I should. But this drum used to belong to her father. He gave it to her with all his hopes and dreams for her life.

(Ta gives Mei-li the drum.)

You can let go of me, Mei-li, but don't let go of this.

(Ta starts to exit.)

MEI-LI: Ta, I heard you were leaving with Linda.
TA: The bus for L.A. left at seven o'clock this morning. The pawn shop didn't open until ten. Good luck to you both.

(Ta exits.)

CHAO: Why didn't you tell me about your drum?
MEI-LI: Because if I had . . . I would never have agreed to go with you.
CHAO: You want to stay where people look at you like you don't belong here? Mei-li, haven't you made enough mistakes?
MEI-LI: No, I can never make enough mistakes.
CHAO: Now you're talking crazy.
MEI-LI: My father made mistakes. But he never stopped believing, even when it cost him his life.
CHAO: Chinese should live where they can be proud to be Chinese.
MEI-LI: I think . . . that's possible here.
CHAO: With him? Maybe he loves you today. But tomorrow, he'll change his mind. Once he decides you're not American enough.

MEI-LI: I'm willing to take that chance.
CHAO: Why?
MEI-LI: Because . . . I believe in him.

(The boat whistles again. Chao looks nervously toward the boat.)

You're making the right choice for you, Chao.
CHAO: 'Til the day I die, I will never understand this.
MEI-LI: I know. That's why you should go.

(Chao exits. Mei-li looks off, then exits in the opposite direction.)

SCENE 7

The theatre. Ta dances his father's role in his re-creation of the opening opera dance. He directs two Warrior Dancers and a Maiden Dancer, none of whom are able to do the Chinese movement well. Unseen by the others, Wang enters and watches his son.

TA:

Along the Hwang Ho Valley,
Where young men walk and dream—

A flower boat with singing girls
Came drifting down the stream.

I saw the face of only one
Come drifting down the stream . . .

You are . . .

(To Maiden Dancer) . . . doing it all wrong.

MAIDEN DANCER: Like anyone in our audience is gonna be able to tell the difference.

TA: If we're gonna do this, let's do it right.

WARRIOR DANCER #1: Why do it at all?

TA: 'Cuz it's a beautiful dance . . . when it's done from the heart. If we want to make something new, we first have to love what is old.

WARRIOR DANCER #2: Oh brother!

(Wang reveals himself.)

WANG: May I?

MAIDEN DANCER: Uncle Sammy? *You* know how to do this old-fashioned stuff?

WANG: I used to. In another life.

(Ta starts to step into his familiar Maiden's role, but Wang takes that position instead.)

TA: Dad! You're really gonna play the girl?

WANG: Someone's got to—if you're ever going to learn to play the man. But I refuse to wear the costume.

(Father and Son dance together.)

You know, Son, it would've been different between us if your mother had lived.

(They dance.)

In so many ways, she was much better than me.

(They dance.)

That's why we did this opera so well together. She always made me feel . . . that I was more than just a man.

TA: The love of a beautiful maiden turned a humble scholar into a god.

(Mei-li enters.)

MEI-LI: No, Ta—you've still got it wrong.

WANG *(To Ta)*: And now, Son, it's your turn.

TA: Guys, take a break.

WANG *(To Dancers)*: Take the day off!

(Wang and Dancers exit, as Mei-li walks up onto the stage with Ta.)

MEI-LI: The love of the Flower Boat Maiden does not turn the scholar into a god. He has always been a god.

TA: But not until he looks into her eyes, does he see his true face.

(Song—"Like a God":)

TA:

> Am I the man that you love?
> If that is true, I am more,
> Something beyond and above,
> The man that I was before.
>
> Like a god
> With my head above the trees,
> I can walk with a god-like stride.
> With a step I can clear the seven seas,
> When I know you are by my side.

Like a god
With a mountain in my hand
And my arm thrown around the sky,
All the world
Can be mine at my command,
When you're near and I hear you sigh.
When you're near and I hear you sigh,
There is no sweeter song I know.
With a heart full of hope I fly,
Higher I go,
Stronger I grow!
Like a god I can tear away the mist
From the sky when you want it blue.
In the wake of the mist
Like a goddess you'll be kissed
By a god in love with you.

(He kisses her.)

MEI-LI: So in America . . . you first date, then marry?
TA: I think we're on our first date.
MEI-LI: Well, I don't like to rush into things. Perhaps we should
date, again.

(She kisses him.)

Now—we must ask my father for his blessing.

(She gets down on her knees, Ta follows.)

MEI-LI *(To heaven)*: Father? There is a young man I want you
to meet.
TA: Master Wu, I am the son of your oldest friend. War and
time have separated you both. But they have also brought

your daughter to me. And now I swear to you, I will do everything in my power—so that when we two are old, at the end of our days—Mei-li will know that she was loved.

MEI-LI: I can almost hear Father, saying to me, "Daughter, you have chosen a man who loves you as much as I do. So now I can let you go."

TA:

> I can tear away the mist
> From the sky when you want it blue.
> In the wake of the mist
> Like a goddess you'll be kissed
> By a god in love with you.

(Mei-li and Ta exit.)

SCENE 8

Months later. The theatre, decorated for a wedding ceremony with a mixture of Chinese and Western motifs. The wedding procession assembles. They speak to the audience.

HARVARD: My parents are still mad at me for not going to some fancy college. But with the money I made here, I bought my mother a watch. Which'll at least help to take some pressure off my little brother—the one they named "Rolex." Anyway, when Madame Liang learned about the wedding, she—

LIANG: —absolutely refused to attend. After all, Ta had quit the club and was performing in Portsmouth Square— with Mei-li—for donations! But ever since Sammy and I got back from our honeymoon, it's like I can't even hold a grudge anymore. One afternoon . . .

WANG: I went to see their show. Which used the traditions of my old opera days to tell new stories—of life in America. Their work reminded me of when I was young, and still believed in impossible things. So I decided to let them hold their wedding here—at the theatre. And once a week—

LIANG: Mondays.

WANG: I would allow Ta and Mei-li to perform a special program here, which we would call . . . opera night.

LINDA: I just landed my first movie role! I play this peasant girl in the Korean War, and when my village gets bombed, I scream. Last week, I got Ta and Mei-li's wedding invitation, and knew I had to come. There are so few people who have what it takes to be happy. The rest of us . . . just stay hungry.

(Chin enters in the robes of a Taoist priest. Mei-li and Ta enter as bride and groom. Chin performs their wedding ceremony.

Song—"A Hundred Million Miracles [Reprise]":)

CHIN:

Om mani padme hum
Om mani padme hum . . .

ALL:

A hundred million miracles

(The groom kisses the bride.)

MEI-LI: As I begin my new life, I give thanks to all those who came before me. My father . . .

TA: . . . my mother, and their ancestors before them . . .

MEI-LI: . . . whose legacy was passed down to me the day I was born *(Turns to face the audience)* in Soochow, China.

TA *(Turns to face the audience)*: The day I was born—in Shanghai.

(As each of the following speak, they step forward to address the audience:)

LINDA: The day I was born—in Seattle.
WANG: In Hunan, China,
HARVARD: In Stockton, California.
LIANG: In New York City.

(Each member of the ensemble now states the actual place of his or her birth. The following represents the Broadway cast, as of opening night on October 17, 2002:)

ELAINE: In Burlington, Ontario.
EMILY: In Providence, Rhode Island.
KIM: In Carlisle, Pennsylvania.
ERICKA: In Ottawa, Canada.
LAINIE: In Oakland, California.
TELLY: In Brooklyn, New York.
DANIEL: In Seoul, Korea.
YUKA: In Okinawa, Japan.
RICH: In Seldon, Long Island.
MARCUS: In Toronto, Canada.
MARC: In Los Angeles, California.
SUSAN: In Honolulu, Hawaii.
ROBERT: In Fremont, California.
ERIC: In Hong Kong.

MEI-LI:

    My father says
    That children keep growing,
    Rivers keep flowing, too.

My father says
He doesn't know why
But, somehow or other, they do.

TA:

They do!
Somehow or other, they do.

MEI-LI AND TA:

A hundred million miracles,
A hundred million miracles
Are happening every day.
And those who say they don't agree,
Are those who do not hear or see.

ALL:

A hundred million miracles,
A hundred million miracles,
A hundred million miracles,
A hundred million miracles
Are happening
Every Day!

(Curtain.)

THE END

✿ AFTERWORD ✿

By Karen Wada

IN 1957, THE YEAR THAT DAVID HENRY HWANG was born, Richard Rodgers and Oscar Hammerstein II decided to turn a new book about San Francisco's Chinatown into a Broadway show. Their choice was a surprise. *The Flower Drum Song* was a first novel by an unknown author named C. Y. Lee, and it featured Asian Americans, a group of people who had never been taken seriously in popular culture. Defying expectations, the stage version became a solid hit, followed by a big-budget movie. Later the musical languished, a victim of changing times.

In 1996, Hwang decided to take another look at *Flower Drum Song*. His choice, too, was a surprise. Why would one of the nation's leading playwrights—and one of Asian America's preeminent figures—dust off such a relic? Once a critic of the work, Hwang had grown to appreciate its pioneering aspects, especially Rodgers and Hammerstein's commitment to presenting Asians as Americans, albeit hokey ones, and to casting

Asian-ancestry actors instead of relying on whites in yellow face. He also came to realize that he was not alone in admitting that *Flower Drum Song* was a guilty pleasure—a source of pride and joy, whatever its flaws. After four decades, the show stands as a rallying point for an often-overlooked minority. The complex reactions it engenders also have made it a lightning rod for the swirling self-images of Asian America.

Mindful of its significance, Hwang knew he needed to go beyond merely updating the play. "I wanted to write what Oscar Hammerstein might have wanted to write if he had been Chinese American," he says. Hwang proposed his ambitious plan to the guardians of the Rodgers and Hammerstein estates and, to the astonishment of many, received permission to do what had never been done before: reconceive one of the duo's works.

This new *Flower Drum Song* had its world premiere in Los Angeles in the fall of 2001. A year later, its arrival in New York was celebrated as a triumph for the now bigger and higher-profile Asian America. However, the fact that this is the first Broadway musical about Asian Americans since the 1958 original illustrates how little has changed on the Great White Way in the half-century since Lee, then an aspiring playwright, was told to write books because the theatre wasn't interested in his "Chinese stuff."

That his characters have ended up onstage anyway, not once but twice, is one of the many coincidences, connections and second chances that mark *Flower Drum Song*'s improbable journey from book to Broadway to Hollywood and back to Broadway. Also remarkable is how the show—and the saga behind it—has touched so many lives and has linked so many of the Asian community's artists and artistic milestones. In effect, it has become a family history of Asian American entertainment, presided over by patriarch Lee.

While some authors might chafe at all the changes that have been made, the wispy-voiced octogenarian says he has welcomed each incarnation of his novel because together they represent the evolution of Asians in America. And while he could have created his own contemporary musical, Hwang says he revisited yesterday's Chinatown because he didn't want to miss out on something special: *"Flower Drum Song* is an extraordinary opportunity to connect the twentieth century of Asian American performers, from C. Y. Lee to the original show to my generation to the kids in our new show."

The story of *Flower Drum Song* begins in Hunan province, where Chin Yang Lee was born in 1917. The youngest son of a rice farmer, he led a picaresque life before fleeing war-torn China on a student visa in the mid-1940s. Although English was definitely a second language, he managed to gain admission to Yale's prestigious playwriting program (to which his first novel is dedicated). "I wanted to study where Eugene O'Neill studied," says Lee, on a recent afternoon at his home in Alhambra, a Los Angeles suburb. At a campus production of one of his plays, Lee met literary agent, Ann Elmo, who invited him to visit her in Manhattan. Being a "country bumpkin," he rushed to the city presuming "fame and fortune were around the corner." What he got was plain—if not prophetic—advice: "Forget that Chinese stuff," Elmo told him, "it will never sell in the American theatre." (There was, and remains, an appetite for tales from Asia. But the stage limited American Asians to playing caricatures of their fringe roles in real life: houseboys, vamps, coolies and crooks.) Elmo encouraged her crestfallen client to try fiction.

Lee headed west, one step ahead of a deportation order because his visa had expired. He rented a room above a honky-tonk in San Francisco's Chinatown and got a job at a small local newspaper, whose peculiar old men inspired several of his characters. One day, he says, he received a call from "an American." Believing he was talking to an immigration officer, he said, "I am packed and ready to go." A startled editor from Writer's Digest replied that Lee had won the magazine's short story contest and $1,500—which was more than a year's pay.

Buoyed by the news, Lee obtained a visa extension and now felt free to start a novel, one that would describe to America the little-known world around him. "I wanted to open a window into Chinese life," he says. He focused on the travails of an obstinately traditional immigrant and his Westernized son. His manuscript was rejected by nearly every publisher in New York, many of them calling it "too quaint." ("That means too Oriental," Lee says.) Finally, Elmo sent *The Flower Drum Song* to Farrar, Straus and Cudahy, her last choice because she considered theirs to be an art house. She told Lee that if he was turned down again he should give up writing. The text went to an outside screener, an elderly man, who after poring over it, scribbled "read this" on the cover, then died in his bed. His bizarre demise prompted John Farrar to examine the book himself. Very impressed, he decided to publish it and became Lee's patron.

The Flower Drum Song (Rodgers and Hammerstein would drop the "The") made the *New York Times* best-seller list in 1957. Lee was hailed as the voice of Chinese America. Some Chinese Americans accused him of pandering to Westerners. "I did write for the mainstream," he says. "I exaggerated a little, but it was all based on what I knew."

Best-seller status prompted a flurry of interest in securing the rights to the book. Elmo narrowed the offers to two. "She called me one morning to congratulate me for picking the right one," Lee says. "I confess that I had had a little to drink the night before so I didn't remember what I had done." Luckily, he had resisted the temptation to take a larger cash sum and agreed to grant an option to producer Joseph Fields for $3,000. Fields squired Lee around Hollywood in hopes of drumming up interest. Among the parties they attended was one at Lana

Turner's home, where Edward G. Robinson came up to the star-struck author and said, "I read your book and I want to play the old man, understand?" Lee went back to San Francisco presuming his favorite actor would appear in a play adapted from his novel.

Then, Fields called with even better news. Rodgers and Hammerstein were interested. "This was the best of the best," Lee says. The creators of *Oklahoma!*, *Carousel*, *South Pacific* and *The King and I* had ruled Broadway for years. When Fields approached them, however, they had suffered disappointment with their last outing, the bittersweet *Pipe Dream*. But once Walter Winchell announced that Rodgers and Hammerstein had a new production in the works, the buzz built quickly, fueled by anticipation that the partners were returning to their beloved ways and speculation about why they were taking a chance on Chinese Americans. Perhaps *Flower Drum Song* satisfied their penchant for pushing liberal values or poking the status quo—a conventional musical showcasing an unconventional subject and cast.

"I think they just liked good stories, and they thought this was one," says Mary Rodgers Guettel, one of the composer's daughters. She adds that her father and Hammerstein did not intend to make history. (Hammerstein later referred to the work as a "lucky" hit.) "Back then people weren't as conscious of what we think about today, race-wise. Daddy and Oscar did know they had to be true to their characters. And they wanted to use Asian people in as many parts as they could because they knew they would look ridiculous otherwise."

Indeed, Rodgers, Hammerstein and Fields embraced two revolutionary ideas: they wanted Asians to play Asians who acted (mostly) like other Americans. Instead of perpetuating the sinister image of Chinatown, then in vogue, they crafted a comfortable (if cardboard) world in which lovers love, parents and children quarrel, and people break into song either soaring or soapy. Their very 1950s storyline lightened up the novel's bleaker themes by featuring a romantic quadrangle among the son, Wang Ta; conniving nightclub singer, Linda Low; her roguish boss, Sammy Fong (a character invented for Broadway); and shy but spunky picture-bride, Mei-li. The father, Master Wang, became a comic foil.

At a time when using white actors in eye makeup was common, *Flower Drum Song* sought out performers of Asian ancestry. This was not easy given immigration limits, industry bias and the fact, as Lee puts it, "That the Chinese didn't encourage their children to act. It was a low profession." Japanese Oscar winner Miyoshi Umeki was signed to play Mei-li. Other roles were harder to fill. The media gushed over the wide-ranging talent hunt (*Time* compared it to "the recruitment of Kublai Khan's harem"). Fields judged a Chinatown beauty pageant. Choreographer Carol Haney stopped potential dancers on the street.

Gene Kelly, who was hired as the director, in part to provide marquee appeal, asked Lee where he could find Asian performers. Lee took him to San Francisco's Forbidden City, the Chinese American answer to Harlem's Cotton Club and a stop on the East-beguiles-West Chop Suey Circuit. There, Kelly discovered comedian Jack Soo, to whom he gave a minor part. (Soo eventually took over the role of Sammy on Broadway and played him in the movie.) For Linda, Hammerstein spotted a tiny sparkplug, Pat Suzuki, belting out songs on a television variety program. She had been working in a small joint near Seattle until she wowed Bing Crosby one night and he helped to launch her career. Honolulu singer Ed Kenney played Ta, and Keye Luke, Charlie Chan's No. 1 son, was Master Wang. The one white lead, Sammy, was stage veteran Larry Blyden (Haney's husband and a late fill-in for comic Larry Storch, who was dropped before the company reached New York). The other non-Asian principal was African American actress Juanita Hall, a Rodgers and Hammerstein favorite from

South Pacific. She portrayed Master Wang's domineering sister-in-law. Among the children was Baayork Lee, who later would appear in the original *A Chorus Line.*

Flower Drum Song opened at the St. James Theatre on December 1, 1958. It ran for six hundred performances and earned a spot in the second tier of Rodgers and Hammerstein hits (which means it's pretty good by anybody else's standard). Rodgers's charming score includes some faux "Oriental" numbers and pop favorites, such as "I Enjoy Being a Girl" (an anthem to being powdered and pampered), the bouncy "Grant Avenue" and "Don't Marry Me" (famously composed at a piano in the ladies' room of an out-of-town theatre) and the haunting ballad "Love Look Away." Hammerstein wrote earnest, if sometimes syrupy, lyrics. His and Fields's libretto, which ranges from clever to corny, is full of mistaken-identity high jinks, pathos, bathos and old-fashioned one-liners.

On opening night, a nervous C. Y. Lee sat with his guests: publisher Farrar and agent Elmo. "The show bowled me over," he says. "I shed tears because it was so good." The reviews were mixed: "Exactly how a perfect show is built" and Kenneth Tynan's "A world of woozy song," a snide reference to *The World of Suzy Wong*, the more typical Anglo Asian romance playing down the street. Being anointed by the nation's top theatre team brought Asian Americans unprecedented news coverage and attention around the country. *Time* profiled Umeki and Suzuki, a Nisei who became the first Asian American to appear on the magazine's cover.

Universal's 1961 *Flower Drum Song* was an even greater showcase, reinforcing lots of stereotypes, but also giving many people their first sight of Chinese as Americans: twirling hula hoops, dancing to rock and roll, courting in convertibles, etc. Fields, working alone because Hammerstein had passed away in the summer of 1960, wrote a script that shuffled the songs and scenes to accelerate the action, which producer Ross

Hunter and director Henry Koster made even splashier and sillier than it had been onstage. Umeki and Soo reprised their roles, but Suzuki was replaced by Nancy Kwan, a ballet student from Hong Kong, who had been plucked from a crowd to star in the film version of *Suzy Wong*. Kwan's looks and legs were big draws for the sexier celluloid *Flower Drum Song*. She and Umeki were pinups; the handsome James Shigeta, the Japanese-Hawaiian actor who played Ta, was that rarity: a singing Asian American leading man.

The rest of the ensemble included—by necessity, because there were so few—almost every recognizable Asian American performer. Among them, Benson Fong (from the Charlie Chan films), Victor Sen Yung (later known as Hop Sing on TV's *Bonanza*) and character actress, Beulah Quo. Hunter reportedly offered Anna May Wong, Hollywood's earliest Chinese-ancestry star, the part of the sister-in-law, but she was too ill to accept, so Hall recreated the role.

"This was the first big movie about Asian Americans," says Kwan, who now lives in Los Angeles. "[Hollywood] spent money on sets, costumes, dance numbers, and they made money. That all said something important." As with the Broadway musical, the reviews for the movie varied wildly. The reaction of Asian Americans was exuberant. The stars were deluged with grateful letters: "They said, it's great to see Asians singing and dancing. Wow!" says Kwan. (Truth be told, some performers' songs were dubbed.) "Flower Drum" restaurants flourished, as did memorabilia-hungry fan clubs. "In San Francisco, I got the key to the city," Lee recalls. "For a long time I never had to buy a meal. It was wonderful."

The story of the latest *Flower Drum Song* begins, in a sense, in nineteenth-century Siam. While watching the 1996 Broadway revival of *The King and I*, David Henry Hwang mused about what other gems he might find in the Rodgers and Hammerstein collection.

Nearly forty years after C. Y. Lee, Hwang enrolled at Yale Drama School. Like Lee, he had wanted to explore the personal and social dramas triggered by assimilation. Unlike Lee, the young Californian had found if not an open theatre, at least a friendlier one. *FOB*, which he had written as a Stanford undergraduate in the late 1970s, was produced by Joseph Papp at New York's Public Theater in 1980. Hwang followed that electrifying debut with a string of plays and movies that established him as a master at blending Western and Asian theatrical styles (a gift later epitomized by his Tony Award-winning *M. Butterfly* in 1988).

Given his professional and personal interests, one Rodgers and Hammerstein show both fascinated him and gave him qualms: "I knew there was a lot to like and not to like about *Flower Drum Song*." Artistically, the Broadway and film versions were confections, examples of old-line musical-comedy rather than the type of integrated musical play Rodgers and Hammerstein had perfected. Culturally, *Flower Drum Song* intrigued and irritated. It was praised for giving Asian Americans rare opportunities offstage and on, and chided for overindulging in exotica. (The *New Yorker* disliked the characters' "childlike sweetness" and sniffed that "there is more than a smidgen of pidgin.")

Everyone was right. Whether seen as patronizing or pioneering, *Flower Drum Song* remains a good barometer of the changing values of Asian America. Older generations, including immigrants who remembered Yellow Peril potboilers, enjoyed this first chance to recognize themselves onscreen. But their American-born children, once they had lived through Vietnam and the Civil Rights Movement, cringed at the pigtailed picture bride and the quaint bits of broken English. Of course, marriages once *were* arranged, and some immigrants do speak with heavy accents. The problem is figuring out when enough "progress" has been made for people to laugh at themselves and feel secure that others will get the joke as well. (Knowing when to laugh certainly became a point of contention for Hwang's *Flower Drum Song*.) This is a tricky calculation for Asian Americans, who care a lot about perceptions, and who also have come to wonder about the costs of being the "model minority." Parents and their Baby Boomer children do share one frustration: they hate being the perpetual outsider, forever presumed to be foreign—and, thus, exotic—no matter how long their families have been in America.

On the other hand, Lea Salonga, the Manila native who played Mei-li in the revival, says she doesn't resent being seen as foreign—because she is. Just don't hold her back because of it. The newer generations of Asian Americans were born abroad or in a relatively more Asian America. (The ghettoized Chinatown of C. Y. Lee's novel is long gone; today, a third of San Francisco's population is of Asian ancestry.) For them, *Flower Drum Song* is interesting "history" but doesn't hit as close to home. However, Salonga, who is in her early thirties, says she has come to understand what this show represents to her American colleagues. One important lesson came a decade ago when she saw the fiery demonstrations against the selection of a white man to play a Eurasian in her first Broadway musical, *Miss Saigon*. The actress, who won a Tony Award for that performance, says she belongs to two worlds, an attitude she thinks strengthened her portrayal of the immigrant heroine, Mei-li.

Aware of all this political baggage, Hwang carefully tested reactions to bringing back *Flower Drum Song*. He found that while a core of criticism persists, most people now dismiss the weak spots as products of their time or more freely concede that they like the play or movie even if they think they shouldn't. MANAA, the Asian American media watchdog, gives the film credit: "Ignore the sitcom plot [and] the corny jokes," its video guide urges, "and relish the sight of some veteran Asian American talent taking the spotlight."

Hwang has acknowledged his own "complicated relationship" with *Flower Drum Song*. While he was in college, he protested against it "almost on principle." Later, he says, especially once he started to work in the theatre, he realized that "you have to look at things in context. I don't think Rodgers and Hammerstein succeeded in creating an authentic Chinese American view of life, but making Asian Americans seem just as American as the characters in *Oklahoma!* is a much more innovative choice." It's also nice, he says, to see Asian American couples in place of the usual white knights matched with faithful (fatally so) Asian women.

"*Flower Drum Song* is *State Fair* in yellow-face," and in this case that's not all bad, says Brown University professor, Robert G. Lee, who has studied the show's role in popular culture. Rodgers and Hammerstein paper over history, whether in Chinatown or small-town Iowa, because they are creating "American-ness." Lee says the key song "Chop Suey" is named for the Chinese dish invented by Americans. Accept that idea and you accept *Flower Drum Song* for what it is.

Aside from societal scrutiny, Hwang knew *Flower Drum* buffs and Rodgers and Hammerstein purists would be watching closely. He also felt the presence of friendly if formidable ghosts: "I realized the authors had a very strong point of view and that it was impossible to change some things. That's because Rodgers and Hammerstein were geniuses of their craft. That's why I feel so fortunate to have had the chance to do so much with their words."

"We trusted him because of his brilliant work," Mary Rodgers Guettel says. "And we knew the show could use some new life."

Hwang confesses that he had trouble with his first drafts. "I went [into the project] somewhat arrogantly," he says, in part because "I'm still fairly new to musicals." To help him turn his rough cuts into smooth song-and-dance he joined up with director-choreographer Robert Longbottom and musical adapter and director David Chase. The trio streamlined the plot, scrapped some of the old characters and melded others together. Songs were reassigned and realigned, and one previously cut from the musical was resurrected.

At the center of it all was Lee's novel, which Hwang considers a neglected classic of Chinese American literature. He says his musical has a twenty-first-century sensibility but echoes the book, especially in its harder edges. While Rodgers, Hammerstein and Fields never went too dark or deep, Lee's melodrama included suicide, vengeful deceit and disillusionment. Hwang created a sleeker, jazzier show, while making references to the Cultural Revolution and the undersides of the immigrant dream.

"I think C. Y. has created something that can be handed down," Hwang says, "in the way *Romeo and Juliet* can become *West Side Story*." Instead of ill-fated lovers, this evolving cycle of stories transforms a battling father and son: Lee's wealthy Master Wang wrestles with Ta, who wrestles with his Chinese and American sides. Rodgers and Hammerstein concocted a stew of comically complicated love affairs. They created a rival (Sammy Fong) for the affections of Linda, whom they turned into both a gold digger interested in Ta's money and a stripper at the Celestial Bar (Celestial Garden in the movie), which they modeled on the Forbidden City.

Hwang completely rewrote the script and injected a modern perspective, often by parodying ethnic stereotypes past and current, and by celebrating, instead of condemning, the campiness of the earlier versions. His Master Wang owns a Chinese opera theatre, which his son wants to turn into a Western nightclub. Although Ta remains smitten with Linda, she has no interest in him. Meanwhile, he spurns Mei-li (at first) because she is too freshly off the boat. Master Wang not only softens his China-centric ways, he becomes an all-American ham with the stage name of Sammy Fong (a nod to the earlier character, who was excised by Hwang; other roles that were given the ax included the sister-in-law and a seamstress, Helen Chao, whose unrequited crush on Ta gave the novel and Rodgers and Hammerstein's musical their bluest notes).

Compared to the 1950s production, casting for the new *Flower Drum Song* was much easier, although the pool of performers was still limited. This time, there was an Asian marquee name—Lea Salonga. Jose Llana, who appeared in *The King and I* revival that piqued Hwang's curiosity, played Ta. Linda was portrayed by saucy Sandra Allen, a Chinese American newcomer, who made it the hard way—through an open call. The distinguished actor Randall Duk Kim was Master Wang. And Jodi Long stole many scenes as a new character, a brassy theatrical agent. Ties to the past were made through Long, whose parents were on the Chop Suey Circuit, and Alvin Ing, who played the young Ta in the first touring company and who now played the elderly uncle Chin.

Some potential backers were wary of the show's old reputation, or had doubts that Asian Americans could sell tickets on Broadway. However, producer Benjamin Mordecai, who had faith in it from the start, brought *Flower Drum Song* to Gordon Davidson, artistic director of the Center Theatre Group in Los Angeles. Davidson also fell in love with the musical and scheduled it to open the spring 2001 season at his Ahmanson Theatre. Then, the intricately arranged funding fell apart and the production was canceled. Unable to let go, Davidson suggested that a leaner version could run at his cozier Mark Taper Forum. Hwang, Longbottom and Chase jumped at the idea. "We actually had been thinking about doing a more intimate show," Hwang says. "The smaller space allowed us to give the drama much more power."

Suddenly, a crisis became a coup. The switch to the Taper gave the play an intensity that no Broadway-scaled musical could match, and enhanced the feeling—apparent to everyone in the house—that this was more than a light night of entertainment. On the first day of rehearsal Hwang reminded the ensemble of not just their own struggles to pursue artistic careers, but the long history of the show and of the community behind it. "No one thought we could make it," he said, "but here we are!"

Flower Drum Song opened on October 14, 2001, and quickly sold out its run. It won glowing reviews for its performances, dance numbers and script. "Daring revision brings out the best in a middling old musical," the *Orange County Register* declared. "The show had a lot of appeal for me on two levels," says Lisa Fung, who oversees drama coverage for the *Los Angeles Times*. "As a first-generation Asian American who grew up in the '60s, I was very familiar with the movie, and, like David, I had a sort of love-hate relationship with the show. As a theatre editor, I found the project to be especially interesting because of the questions it raised: how would the revisions address some of the show's negative Asian stereotypes? How would it play to non-Asian audiences? Would it offend Asian audiences? Dealing with the stereotypes through humor appeared to give everyone in the audience permission to relax and enjoy other aspects of the musical as a whole."

The rousing reception from theatre critics and playgoers helped to ensure that *Flower Drum Song* got the financial support it needed to move to New York. In preparation, the company began to fine-tune the script. "We felt the show was about eighty percent of where we wanted it to be, in all departments," says Hwang. He and Longbottom sharpened the storytelling, deepened the character conflicts and opened up the production numbers.

On October 17, 2002, *Flower Drum Song* was back on Broadway. The musical was praised in reviews like the *New*

Yorker's, which dubbed it, "Part fashion show, part night-club act, part hymn to Asian American diversity," and deemed it to be better than the original. Others, notably the *New York Times*, said that in remaking itself, the production had lost its identity; some said it also had succumbed to the sexism and exoticism it had set out to remedy. Such complaints were countered by claims, often by Asian Americans, that the naysayers misunderstood Hwang's intentions, or represented what *Time* called a "gauntlet of critics suddenly quite protective of a musical they never much liked in the first place."

It is inevitable that defining the soul of *Flower Drum Song* would provoke such debate. After all, identity questions are a crucial part of the Asian American experience, and are what inspired both Lee and Hwang to become writers. Besides, this show is an Asian American's take on three Anglo Americans' take on an Asian-immigrant's take on America. That's a tangled layering of plots and politics, made even more tangled because Hwang tried to capture the spirit of the old, amid expectations that he create something strikingly new. "*Flower Drum Song* achieves exactly what I dreamed of accomplishing when I first envisioned remaking it," Hwang says. "I wanted to marry the heart and fun of a classic '40s or '50s musical with the cultural values of today." Such a marriage is tricky, given the volatility of evolving ethnicity and the fact that Hwang chose humor—so slyly effective and yet so easy to miss or to misperceive—to make many of his points. What, then, should we take at face value, and what is meant to be read with asterisks or arched eyebrows?

"Chop Suey" is a key to understanding this new *Flower Drum Song* as well as the old one. In their deliberately over-the-top version, Hwang and Longbottom present a kaleidoscope of scantily clad chorines who don oversized Chinese takeout-food boxes. This is not an attempt, as some critics say, to have one's cheesecake and eat it too. It's done just for fun, as satire (ah, Asian women as tasty dishes), and as an homage to the classic musicals of the past.

More subtly, Asians and non-Asians can appreciate moments that transcend race and yet carry a special kick because of it, like watching a great performance of a great role—as happens when Jodi Long milks the most out of her character. By playing the agent as a Chinese Ethel Merman, she honors a theatre tradition, while busting an ethnic stereotype (an Asian with chutzpah!).

Six months after it opened, *Flower Drum Song* put up its closing notices, dogged by the sluggish economy, post-September 11 jitters, the *New York Times*' mixed review, and unusually bitter winter weather. Most important, the show never gained the momentum—cross-over or otherwise—it needed to establish itself as a must-see hit. "We also got caught in the zeitgeist," Hwang says. "People were into irony, and while we had our share of that we also were trying to be more sincere than many of the other things running on Broadway."

The final curtain came down at the Virginia Theatre on March 16, 2003. Hwang hopes *Flower Drum Song*'s premature end won't validate the doubts of those who suspect shows with Asian American themes cannot carry their weight in commercial theatre. "The fact that we got [to Broadway]," he says, "and had a good run will, I think, inspire others—perhaps even from within the Asian American community itself—to invest in the future."

He was touched by the excitement of Asian Americans who watched this *Flower Drum Song* and "who came back with their children and grandparents." They reminded him "of how rare it is for us to attend a mainstream cultural event where we feel included, where we can laugh, and feel entertained, and maybe a little bit moved, just like anybody else. After that kind of experience I think there is no turning back."

He would like to see his libretto join the official Rodgers and Hammerstein repertoire. Theodore S. Chapin, president of the Rodgers and Hammerstein Organization, affirms his group's enthusiasm for Hwang's script and predicts an increase in productions of *Flower Drum Song*, which was infrequently staged after the early '60s. (The movie, which lives on through cable and video, has become the best-known face of *Flower Drum Song* and the version most Asian Americans have come to love or, at least, secretly appreciate.)

The national tour of the new *Flower Drum Song* is scheduled to open in Dallas in the fall of 2003. Plans for an international run are under discussion.

The Broadway revival has reignited interest in the work of C. Y. Lee, who has written nearly a dozen books since *The Flower Drum Song*. Lee is returning to a long-delayed dream of his own: he is writing a musical.

Hwang also is contemplating creating a new musical with an Asian American cast and theme: "I think we'd all hate to think that it will take forty years more to see a show like this on Broadway."

"With our *Flower Drum Song* we pushed one boulder up the hill," Hwang says. "Maybe I'll try to push another one!"

March 2003
Los Angeles

Karen Wada is a senior editor at *Los Angeles* magazine, where she also writes about subjects including culture and theatre. Previously, she worked on daily newspapers for twenty-five years, including two decades at the *Los Angeles Times*, where she served as one of the paper's managing editors, overseeing international and national news and editing showcase features and projects. Wada has written for a number of national arts and news publications. She lives with her husband Clark and daughter Gwen near Los Angeles.

Portions of this article appeared in another version in *Los Angeles* magazine.

RICHARD RODGERS (1902–1979; composer) and **OSCAR HAMMERSTEIN II** (1895–1960; lyricist, original co-librettist) After distinguished careers with other collaborators, Richard Rodgers and Oscar Hammerstein II joined forces in 1943 to create the most successful partnership in the American musical theatre. *Oklahoma!*, the first Rodgers and Hammerstein musical, was followed by *Carousel* (1945), the movie *State Fair* (1945; remade 1962; Broadway premiere, 1996), *Allegro* (1947), *South Pacific* (1949), *The King and I* (1951), *Me and Juliet* (1953), *Pipe Dream* (1955), the TV musical *Cinderella* (1957; remade 1965, 1997), *Flower Drum Song* (1958) and *The Sound of Music* (1959).

JOSEPH FIELDS (1895–1966; original co-librettist) wrote or co-authored the stage hits *My Sister Eileen*, *Junior Miss*, *Anniversary Waltz*, *Wonderful Town*, *Gentlemen Prefer Blondes*, *Tunnel of Love* and *Flower Drum Song*, for which he also wrote the screenplay. He also wrote and/or produced numerous films, including the Marx Brothers' *Night in Casablanca* and *Annie Oakley*.

DAVID HENRY HWANG was awarded the 1988 Tony, Drama Desk, Outer Critics and John Gassner Awards for his Broadway debut, *M. Butterfly*, which was also a finalist for the Pulitzer Prize. For his most recent play, *Golden Child*, he received a 1998 Tony nomination and a 1997 OBIE Award. He also co-authored the book for Elton John and Tim Rice's *Aida*, winner of four 2000 Tony Awards. Other plays include *FOB* (1981 OBIE Award): *The Dance and the Railroad*, *Family Devotions*, *The Sound of a Voice* (all produced by The Joseph Papp Public Theater/New York Shakespeare Festival) and *Bondage* (Actors Theatre of Louisville). His opera libretti include three works by composer Philip Glass: *1000 Airplanes on the Roof* (International Tour), *The Voyage* (Metropolitan Opera) and *The Sound of a Voice* (American Repertory Theatre); as well as *The Silver River* with music by Bright Sheng (Lincoln Center Festival); and *Ainadamar* with music by Osvaldo Golijov (Tanglewood Music Center). Mr. Hwang penned the feature films *M. Butterfly*, *Golden Gate* and *Possession* (co-writer). He serves on The Dramatists Guild Council.